ADVERTISING, ALCOHOL CONSUMPTION, AND MORTALITY

ADVERTISING, ALCOHOL CONSUMPTION, AND MORTALITY

An Empirical Investigation

Joseph C. Fisher
and Peter A. Cook

Contributions to the Study of Mass Media and Communications,
Number 47

GREENWOOD PRESS
Westport, Connecticut • London

659.1
F53a

Library of Congress Cataloging-in-Publication Data

Fisher, Joseph C.
    Advertising, alcohol consumption, and mortality : an empirical investigation / Joseph
C. Fisher, Peter A. Cook.
        p.   cm.—(Contributions to the study of mass media and communications, ISSN
0732–4456; no. 47)
    Includes bibliographical references and index.
    ISBN 0–313–29457–7 (alk. paper)
    1. Advertising—Alcoholic beverages—United States.   2. Drinking
of alcoholic beverages—United States.   3. Alcoholism—United
States.   I. Cook, Peter A.   II. Title.
    HF6161.L46F57   1995
    659.1'96631'0973—dc20   95–9874

British Library Cataloguing in Publication Data is available.

Library of Congress Catalog Card Number: 95–9874
ISBN: 0–313–29457–7
ISSN: 0732–4456

First published in 1995

Greenwood Press, 88 Post Road West, Westport, CT 06881
An imprint of Greenwood Publishing Group, Inc.

Printed in the United States of America

The paper used in this book complies with the
Permanent Paper Standard issued by the National
Information Standards Organization (Z39.48–1984).

10   9   8   7   6   5   4   3   2   1

For
Dorit, Jacob, and Jane
and
Edna and Leslie Cook

Contents

Figures and Tables

Preface

A decade ago Lawrence Wallack wrote a provocative article in which he argued, "the issue of whether advertising directly increases the consumption of alcoholic beverages is irrelevant both from a regulatory and a public health perspective" (Wallack, 1984, p. 98). The regulatory question, he maintained, should be concerned only with whether alcoholic beverage advertising is deceptive and misleading since drinking is not associated with personal, social, and sexual success as frequently portrayed in commercials. Whether advertising should be permitted at all for products whose consumption can lead to social and health problems, he suggested, is the central public health question.

Wallack's article marks a subtle yet crucial paradigm shift in the field. The consequences of advertising as manifest in observable, measurable consumer behavior no longer matter. Ads themselves, their content, themes, and tone instead become the object of study. Criticisms of lifestyle advertising are a direct result. The research focus is redirected almost imperceptibly from the realm of demonstrable evidence to a more subjective one in which assessments of advertising impacts are based on the perspective of the evaluator. Effects are in the eye of the beholder not the actions of buyers.

The research reported in this book was predicated on precisely the opposite view. Effects are not only relevant they are crucial to understanding where, when, and how advertising works as well as what the public health consequences and implications of alcoholic beverage advertising are. Effects are central to policy-making, we believe, if for no other reason than the likely consequences of one regulatory option can be evaluated in relation to competing alternatives. In the extreme, the presence or absence of effects can help determine if regulation is warranted at all.

In our research over the last fifteen years we have evaluated scores of advertising campaigns and promotional programs, for large and small companies alike. We are convinced that advertising is a powerful force in the marketplace and is a cost-effective means of influencing consumer behavior. We are also convinced that advertising effects are real and empirically measurable. When they are not seen in an analysis, we tend to accept the simplest explanation, none were present in a given situation, rather than conclude effects are of no consequence.

Of course, even the most objective findings must ultimately be subjectively evaluated. Social scientists do not work in a political vacuum and the interpretation of results often reflects a value orientation either implicitly held or explicitly acknowledged. The financial exigencies of conducting research can also shape the investigation. The interests of funding sources determine the questions that will be considered and how the study will be conducted and influence the tone and direction the discussion of findings will take.

This fact has not gone unnoticed by those commenting on the state of research in the field. Wallack (1992), as an example, suggested that studies funded by alcoholic beverage manufacturers rarely come to conclusions that are inconsistent with manufacturers' interests. One of us (Fisher, 1993) similarly observed that government-funded investigators interpret findings in a manner that furthers the policy mandate and objectives of the granting agency.

In this regard it is important to state that the study reported here was entirely self-funded by the authors. The investigation originated from our own curiosity, was designed to meet our ends, data were analyzed to the best of our ability, and results were interpreted according to what we alone believed them to show. We are solely responsible for any errors or omissions.

This is not to say we did not have help during the investigation and, indeed, there are many individuals and organizations to whom we are indebted. Competitive Media Research graciously gave us access to their media tracking reports. Ms. Lucy Aleman was particularly important in helping us gain permission to use the data. John Ciotoli was always willing to share his time and expertise as we assembled data and attempted to interpret it.

Our good friend and colleague, Dr. Thomas Harford, Director of Biometry and Epidemiology for the National Institute of Alcohol Abuse and Alcoholism, also provided invaluable assistance during the data collection phase of the project. Tom is one of the rare individuals who quietly and unselfishly makes a continuing contribution to the field and the researchers in it. We appreciate his support of this project and others in the past.

Working under Tom's direction are a number of individuals whose professional attention to detail made our task immeasurably easier. Dr. Gale Savage of Cygnus Corporation and Drs. Gerald Williams and Frederick Stinson of CSR, Inc., were instrumental in compiling per capita alcohol consumption figures and liver cirrhosis mortality statistics used throughout the research. Each of these individuals took the time to share their insiders' knowledge of the data with us.

We also benefited from considerable assistance in our own organization,

InterData, Inc., Susan Warstadt, Javeed Ismail, and Craig Tomarkin helped with library research, statistical analysis, and in the preparation of the text. Marty Krasnick identified where we could obtain media data and helped negotiate access to it. The majority of the library research as well as the data compilation and construction of the analytic files was accomplished by our summer intern, William Thompson, and we are grateful for his perseverance and hard work.

Most of all we had the tireless support of our families; the Fishers: Dorit, Jacob, and Jane, who provided encouragement and accepted the nights and weekends lost to this endeavor; Edna and Leslie Cook whose example taught the consultant's traits of listening, assisting, and supporting; and Judy, Margaret, and Catherine Cook for their assistance and support. All have our lasting love and gratitude.

Chapter 1

Introduction

The advertising of alcoholic beverage products is a subject of vehement public debate and prospective policy-making. Commercials are criticized for their ubiquity, frequency, contents and cost. Manufacturers' motives for using advertising are questioned and presumed to be aimed toward unrelenting market expansion and to precondition a new generation of adolescents to become inveterate drinkers.[1] In response, efforts are made to curtail advertising by restricting media venues, limiting placement options, and minimizing creative freedom or to make advertising less attractive for manufacturers by eliminating its deductibility as a business expense.

As the most public marketing tool available to manufacturers, advertising, almost inevitably, will come under public scrutiny and become the target of public health advocates who seek to limit alcohol consumption. But the question remains—does advertising in reality cause people to drink more than they otherwise would? If so, does the extra quantity of alcohol consumed finally find expression in elevated rates of alcohol-related social problems and disease? In the crudest financial terms, is the American public paying for manufacturers' profits in the form of higher medical care costs?

The study reported here was designed to address questions such as these in an empirical context. We have attempted to make explicit the assumptions held by those who believe advertising leads to increased consumption and concomitant disease, and to test their validity. Our goal is to assess the impact alcoholic beverage advertising has on the amount of alcohol Americans consume each year and to determine, to the degree possible, if the amount of consumption attributable to advertising can be shown to affect mortality from prototypic alcohol-related diseases.

LITERATURE REVIEW

In many respects this study is an outgrowth of a worldwide survey of the scientific literature conducted several years ago (Fisher, 1993). The original investigation had as its goal the compilation and interpretation of scientific, that is to say empirical, studies that would address the question—does advertising for alcohol products measurably affect alcohol consumption or adverse outcomes associated with drinking? The objective of the review was posed therefore as a test of the null hypothesis—advertising does not influence alcohol consumption and has no impact on alcohol abuse or alcohol-related disease and death.

Almost immediately it became clear that a simple chain of causality was assumed, either implicitly or explicitly, by researchers to explain how advertising could affect behavior (Figure 1.1). Exposure to alcohol messages in the media was expected to initiate, stimulate, or perpetuate drinking. Next the resulting increased consumption was expected, eventually, to be manifest as elevated rates of negative outcomes associated with excessive drinking such as increased morbidity and mortality from alcohol-related disease.

Two theoretical traditions were employed to form the links in the chain. Typically, social learning theory was invoked to supply the rationale to explain how drinking behavior would be acquired or influenced after exposure to alcohol images. Social learning theory is an operant conditioning model and posits that behavior is caused by the consequences that follow it. Of particular importance in the theory are actual experiences with alcohol and what happens during and after these drinking occasions, known theoretically as differential reinforcement.

What sets social learning theory apart from a pure operant conditioning model though is the belief that complex behavior is learned in interaction with significant others through a process known as differential association. Parents and peers provide definitions of the behavior and models for acceptable use and ultimately the definitions and attitudes about the behavior are internalized and become self-reinforcing. The summated effect of differential reinforcement and differential association, unique for every individual, determines how alcohol will be used and whether or not it will be used abusively.

Another tenet of social learning theory is especially important in explaining how media affects behavior. Applying the results of Albert Bandura's (Bandura et al., 1963; Bandura, 1965) seminal social psychological experiments on aggression in preschoolers to the alcohol field, researchers have suggested that drinking can be learned not only in interaction with significant others but additionally by watching filmed models, in the extreme even cartoon figures. The observer can learn by seeing the consequences that befall the filmed models when they drink. According to Bandura's results behavior is more likely if positive or neutral (non-negative) consequences follow the actions of the model and is less likely only when the consequences are negative.

It is impossible to overstate how important Bandura's work and the belief in learning through imitation is to the explanations of advertising effects given in

Figure 1.1
Theoretical Basis for Advertising Effects

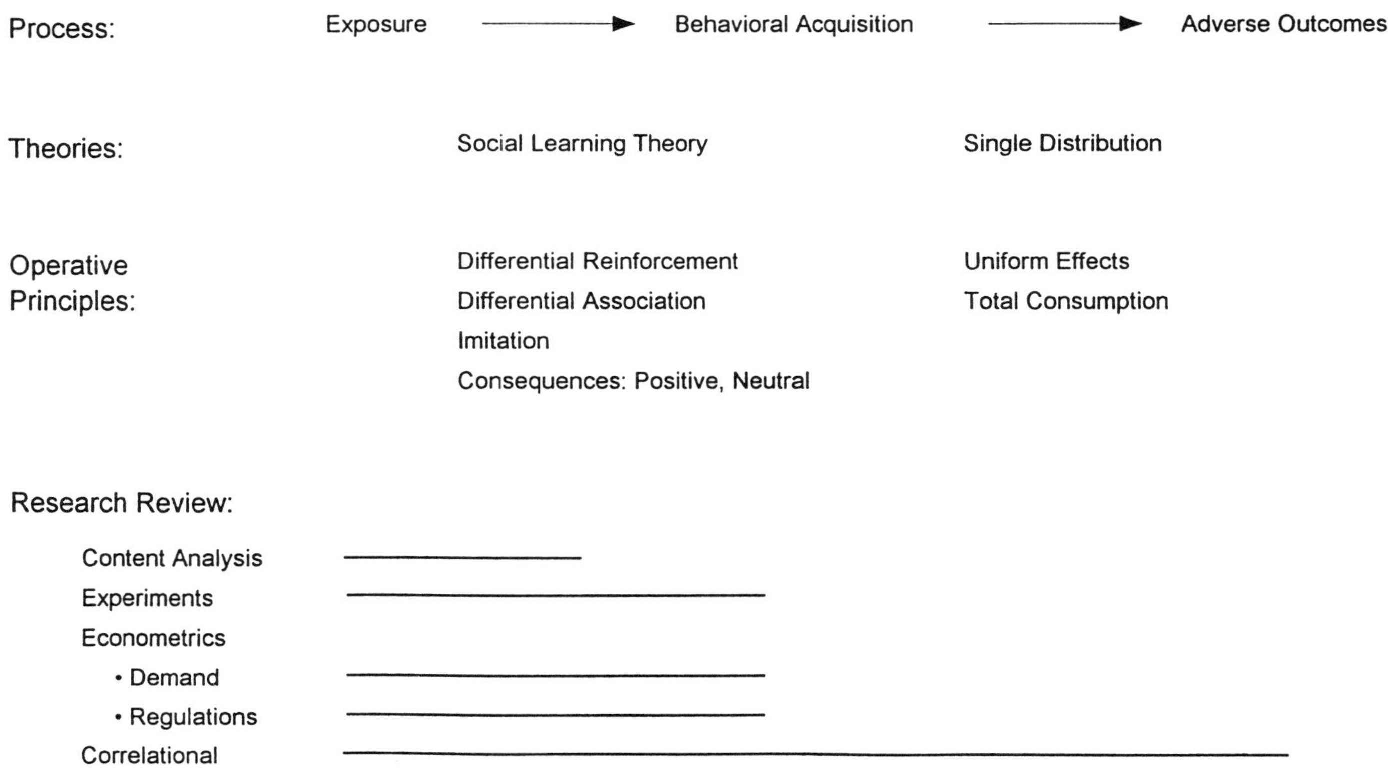

Process:	Exposure	───▶	Behavioral Acquisition	───▶	Adverse Outcomes

Theories:

                    Social Learning Theory   Single Distribution

Operative
Principles:

                    Differential Reinforcement   Uniform Effects
                    Differential Association   Total Consumption
                    Imitation
                    Consequences: Positive, Neutral

Research Review:

    Content Analysis   ————————

    Experiments   ————————

    Econometrics

      • Demand   ————————

      • Regulations   ————————

    Correlational   ————————————————

the literature. For example, content analysis studies of the media routinely count the number of alcohol messages to which viewers are exposed. Efforts are also made to categorize the tone of the image; do drinkers receive rewards or positive benefits for their actions, no consequences, or negative reinforcement? Since the majority of images are thought to portray positive or neutral consequences, it is assumed, on theoretical grounds without the benefit of empirical support, that alcohol images in programming and commercials promote increased consumption.

The second theory employed in the literature to connect behavior and adverse outcomes is the single distribution of alcoholism prevalence. This theory suggests that the distribution of alcohol consumption in a population is lognormal and that the rate of alcohol-related morbidity and mortality is a function of the mean of the distribution, that is, the average per capita consumption, and the percentage of the population in the tail of the distribution that drink excessively. Any external influence, potentially advertising, that increases the mean per capita consumption or enlarges the proportion of the population who drink to excess will elevate rates of alcohol-related adverse outcomes therefore.

The single distribution theory is relevant to the discussion of media effects not only because advertising is assumed to be one of the external influences that raises the mean level of consumption, but also because of the specific type of effect on consumption that must be observed for adverse outcomes to result. Specifically, the *total* amount of *absolute* alcohol per capita must increase. It is not sufficient for the sales of one brand to increase or for that matter consumption of a category of beverage such as liquor to rise, since the increase in one brand or category may be offset by declines in consumption of a competitive brand or substitute beverage type. Only when total consumption increases are concomitant increases in adverse outcomes predicted.

And there in lies the rub. Most researchers are not clear in their thinking regarding how alcohol advertising affects total consumption. Brand level effects are confused with category level influences and ultimately the impact of advertising on total consumption. More to the point, few studies look at the entire system of alcoholic beverage consumption content only to examine brand or less often category effects. However, it is important to note that demonstrating advertising affects brand or category consumption does not necessarily imply that adverse outcomes will result since no effect on total consumption is observed.

The confusion regarding the single distribution theory and how advertising works helps also, we think, explain one of the issues that seems to mystify social scientists—how it is possible to reconcile the body of scientific evidence showing no relationship between advertising and consumption with the huge sums manufacturers spend annually to advertise their products. In short, why would manufacturers continue to advertise unless there was an increase in consumption the profits from which more than offset the advertising investment. Of course, the answer to the apparent paradox is that both sides of the argument are probably true. Virtually all advertising is at the brand level and it does shift product shares and increase brand sales far in excess of the amount expended on advertising. Quite simply advertising makes good financial sense for manufacturers. On the other hand, gains in sales of one brand, especially in a static or mature market, are obtained at the expense of a competitive product, and the net effect on total consumption in the end is nil.

The single distribution theory has other implications for the study of media effects. The theory is something of a black box in that it is irrelevant how advertising works as long as it can be shown to affect total consumption. Advertising might affect all individuals uniformly or it might differentially impact at-risk groups. Regardless, when it comes to predicting negative outcomes only total consumption per capita matters. In a sense then the single distribution theory is seductively simple and leads us away from a complex view of advertising effects and the potential for differential impact among consumer subpopulations.

Social learning theory and the single distribution theory inform much of the scientific literature regarding advertising and alcohol consumption, therefore, in terms of what issues are investigated, the way studies are designed, and how results are interpreted. Using these theories as background a variety of disciplines and methodologies have attempted to address some or all of the causal chain. When we examine the empirical literature it falls neatly into several generic forms of investigation: content analyses, experiments, econometric studies of demand, evaluations of changes in permissible advertising, and quasi-experimental or correlational studies. The major findings from each of these areas will be considered in turn.

The content analytic method is meant to measure and describe the number of alcohol images to which the population is exposed. To this end attempts are made to count the number of alcohol messages that are conveyed in the media and to characterize their intent, tonality, and likely impact on behavior. Presumably, consumption will increase with exposure to alcohol images and if, as suggested by social learning theory, the consequences associated with the occurrences are disproportionally positive or neutral. Virtually every form of artistic expression has been the subject of content analysis, including fictional literature, popular, country and western, and blues music, and films. But the majority of the work has concentrated on the most influential and persuasive medium, television.

Taken as a whole, a number of conclusions seem warranted from content analyses. Regardless of the medium, alcohol images have become more commonplace over time both in terms of the frequency with which the images occur and the way alcohol is used. Second, alcohol use in the media appears to reflect the social mores of the era, while at the same time images tend to explore the limits of acceptable behavior.

With respect to television, roughly two-thirds of all prime time shows depict a character drinking. Additionally, alcohol is shown at the rate of 8 times per hour during prime time programs and is ingested by a character 2.4 times per hour. Projecting these figures to a year of viewing, a person in the United States who watched three hours of prime time television every weekday would be exposed to 6,240 alcohol depictions per year and actually observe alcohol consumed 1,872 times. Interestingly, the frequency with which alcohol images are seen in programming and the rates per hour are consistent with those obtained in studies of programming outside the United States.

Prime time television, of course, tends to be the most dramatic programming and have exceptionally high rates of alcohol portrayals. When a representative sample of television programming was analyzed (Cafiso et al., 1982), it was found that alcohol images appeared at the rate of 3.6 times per hour and the rate was not very different than the rate of 2.9 times per hour for nonalcoholic beverages. With respect to commercials, ads for alcoholic beverages occurred .6 times per hour or roughly one-sixth as often as an alcohol image in programming. They were also about 5 times less frequent than ads for nonalcoholic beverages that appeared 2.8 times per hour. Again, our hypothetical viewer of three hours of television every weekday might encounter, on average, 468 ads for alcohol products throughout the year.

The content analysis tradition has been valuable in benchmarking the extent of alcohol messages in the media and tracking trends in the number and rates of portrayals over time. It is clear from the research that the messages are numerous and ubiquitous. It is also apparent that the vast majority of alcohol images are conveyed as part of normal programming and not in the form of commercial appeals. What is not possible to determine from content analyses is how the ambient media climate with alcohol images embedded influences behavior. Other forms of investigation are required and Figure 1.2 summarizes the other methodologies that have been employed and the collective findings.

Experiments typically vary the degree of exposure given to various groups and subsequently observe their drinking behavior or intentions to drink or purchase. The prototypic experiment might, as an example, vary the number of ads seen, such as, 0, 4, 9, or the way alcohol images were conveyed, programs versus ads, or compare alcohol ad exposure with exposure to ads for nonalcoholic beverages. During the experiment subjects might be allowed to order drinks from an open bar or after it may be asked to fill out a rating scale. Differences in consumption or intention between treatment groups is assumed to be a result of variations in exposure.

The experimental method has the advantage of enabling the investigator to manipulate exposure directly and hence when differences are observed causality is clear cut. The problem is advertising effects are never observed. Regardless of how experiments are designed, and some are quite creative (see Kohn et al., 1984, as an example), or how outcomes are measured, exposure to advertising has not been shown to be significantly related to consumption or intentions among normal drinkers. Surprisingly, this conclusion does not hold for alcoholics in treatment who have been exposed to alcohol ads (Fisher, 1980; Sobell

Figure 1.2
Summary of Empirical Findings

	Advertising Effect	Comment
Experiments		
Normal Drinkers	0	No Effect
Alcoholics	–	Strong paradoxical effect, counterargue persuasive appeals
Quasi Experiments		
Experimentation	0	No Effect on trial
Consumption	+	Weak positive impact and possible reinforcement of drinking
Abuse	0	No direct effect, very small indirect through consumption
Econometric		
US	0	No effect in better studies and when demography controlled
Canada	0	No effect or counterintuitive findings
Foreign	+	Weak relationship, 10:1 ratio, effects on total consumption dissipate systemwide
Advertising Regulations	0	No evidence consumption patterns are affected by changes in permissible advertising

From Fisher (1993)

et al., 1993). These individuals apparently recognize the ad as persuasive communication and attempt to protect themselves by counterarguing the appeal. Nevertheless on-balance experiments have been unable to link advertising exposure to drinking behavior.

The experimental method may, however, not be well suited to observe advertising effects. If we suppose that advertising effects are cumulative and take considerable time to develop a simple two-hour experiment, during which at most nine ads are shown, would be hopelessly inadequate to measure any lasting impact. Further, ethical imperatives often constrain the studies, for instance, by limiting the number of drinks an individual can be served.

The quasi-experimental tradition overcomes many of these shortcomings but at the expense of less certainty concerning causality. In the typical quasi-experimental study a group of individuals, most often teenagers, are surveyed. The questionnaire administered queries respondents about their media usage habits, use and abuse of alcohol as well as a variety of presumed covariates such as parental and peer drinking or demographics. Media data are used to estimate the amount of alcohol advertising exposure and this figure is then correlated with drinking behavior and indicators of abuse. The chief advantage of the survey approach is that the entire chain of causality, exposure to consumption to abuse, can be examined, albeit in a correlational manner.

There are precious few quasi-experiments reported in the literature. Despite the relatively small number, the results are remarkably similar across studies. None of the studies has found a significant effect for imitation thereby calling into question one of the major operative mechanisms proposed by social learning theory to explain how advertising influences behavior. Second, no significant advertising effects on trial have been observed thus calling into question the ability of advertising to initiate drinking. Advertising was shown to be weakly associated with consumption; specifically between .2 to 4% of the variability in alcohol consumption could be explained by advertising exposure when other factors were held constant. Advertising was even more tenuously associated with indicators of abuse. It explained only between .2 to 1.2% of the variance in the frequency of intoxication and between .1 to 1.2% in other measures of abuse such as psychological involvement, drinking and driving or self-reported problems. Moreover, advertising effects were not direct but only operated indirectly through consumption.

Quasi-experiments have also demonstrated what may be reinforcing effects for advertising. In particular, a number of studies have shown that the greater the involvement with alcohol, the more likely teenagers are to be aware of alcohol ads, recognize brands and slogans, and find alcohol ads appealing. And yet, quasi-experiments are inherently static in that a single measurement is taken at a point in time. Survey responses are correlated and causality is more often than not in the mind of the investigator. It is possible then that those who drink more or are pathologically involved with alcohol are more likely to notice and remember alcohol advertising. So while reinforcement of behavior may be a very real effect of advertising, it cannot be unambiguously observed or accurately measured with a survey instrument.

Econometric studies frequently take a dynamic approach and attempt to estimate demand for alcoholic beverages by analyzing consumption patterns over time. The basic demand model consists of a measure of demand (income) and supply (price) and for our purposes it must contain an advertising variable. Other predictors of demand such as demographic or social factors can also be included at the discretion of the investigator. These demand determinants are subsequently related to indicators of consumption, such as sales, expenditures or volumetric data, in a regression or time series context.

Generally, the results of econometric analyses, like those for quasi-experiments, show weak relationships between advertising and consumption. In fact, studies conducted using U.S. data have shown no effect when demographic factors are controlled, while those using Canadian data are equally unproductive. The principal limitation of these studies has been the fact that they usually concentrate on brand or category consumption and do not investigate advertising effects on the full system of alcoholic beverage consumption options. As such, they do not provide evidence that is required by the single distribution theory.

Perhaps the best econometric research is done outside North America, most noticeably in the United Kingdom. After extensive analysis and reanalysis of two overlapping data sets, investigators have arrived at several conclusions regarding how advertising affects consumption. First, there seems to be a weak relationship such that a 10% increase in advertising for a product category, for example, beer, will produce a 1% increase in consumption for the category. Second, beverage types are to a considerable degree substitutes for one another so that increases in consumption for one category will be offset by reduced consumption of another. As a consequence, advertising effects tend to dampen across the full range of product options and hence the net effect on total consumption is minimal.

The last body of evidence, and perhaps the most persuasive, comes from evaluations of changes in permissible advertising. These studies are made possible when a geopolitical region, state, or province either bans some form of alcohol advertising or permits advertising after it has been banned. By comparing consumption of alcohol before and after the change in policy with similar data from a control region it is possible to determine whether variations in advertising affect consumer behavior in any discernible manner.

Almost all of the work in this area has been evaluations of changes in Canadian law. Without exception no study has been able to document a significant change in consumption as a function of a mandated change in permissible advertising. The evaluations are not perfect, Canada is after all influenced by American media and spill-over advertising from the United States. Nevertheless, the failure to find any affect on consumption after advertising has been banned or permitted after a ban is possibly the most compelling evidence that advertising does not affect total consumption.

Reviewing the findings and conclusions of the entire body of research, across numerous studies conducted by a variety of disciplines and employing a wide range of methodology, there does not seem to be strong support for the notion that advertising affects alcohol consumption in a meaningful way. As a consequence, the literature review concluded that the null hypothesis should be accepted and that, "in the end, there seems to be little reason to believe advertising increases consumption to the point that meaningful adverse social consequences result" (Fisher, 1993, p. 151). The goal of this study is to determine if this conclusion is still warranted when the hypothesis is explicitly stated and tested empirically.

RECENT RESEARCH

There have been no empirical studies published in the literature since the worldwide survey was conducted that would alter its conclusions in any way. For example, a recent content analysis (Madden and Grube, 1994) investigated alcohol and tobacco advertising on sports programming during 1990 through 1992. In all 443.7 hours of broadcasting were analyzed, which included 35 college, 66 professional sports events (mostly football), and 65 other televised sports contests such as golf, auto racing, bicycling, and the Olympics.

A total of 685 commercials for alcoholic beverages were broadcast during the events studied and these represented 77% of all beverage commercials. By comparison, commercials for nonalcoholic beers appeared only 39 times or one-twentieth as often. Moderation messages and public service announcements (PSAs) were even less frequently broadcast. Only 3 of the 685 alcohol ads were paired with a moderation message while just 10 PSAs were observed.

As for rates, the authors found that there were 1.54 ads for alcoholic beverage products for every hour of programming or roughly two and a half times the rate of .62 ads per hour obtained when all television programming was analyzed (Cafiso et al., 1982). Additionally, the investigators found that there were 3.3 nonstandard ads per hour, where a nonstandard ad was defined as the appearance on camera of stadium signs advertising an alcohol product. The ads, in turn, were deemed to promote drinking and possibly abuse, since 15% used celebrity endorsers, 16% contained images of cars, and 26% activities around water. From these data, the authors concluded:

These images or themes are at odds with former Surgeon General Koop's 1989 recommendations that alcohol advertising not portray activities that are dangerous when combined with drinking and that such advertising avoid celebrity endorsers, especially those who appeal to young people. Viewers are also exposed to alcohol advertising via stadium signs, other on-site promotions, and brief product sponsorships. Moderation messages and public service announcements to alcohol are rarely broadcast. Thus, sports viewers receive primarily positive messages about drinking. (Madden and Grube, 1994, p. 299)

The social learning orientation of the authors is clearly evident in the quotation as is the assumption that since advertising portrays positive images of alcohol products it must therefore promote drinking. However, like all content analyses there is no evidence presented that those who are exposed to the ads drink more or more abusively than those who did not see the ads. In the end, it is difficult to know exactly how to assess the practical import of a study such as this. Perhaps its greatest value is benchmarking a type of programming that has not often been studied and expanding the review and analysis to include nonstandard forms of advertising, forms of communication that are absorbing increasingly large shares of manufacturers' marketing budgets.

In a follow-on and more predictive study of fifth- and sixth-graders Grube and Wallack (1994) attempted to relate advertising awareness to intentions to drink as adults. A total of 468 children, ethnically mixed and about evenly split between males and females, took part in the study. Participants were queried about their television viewing, awareness of beer advertising, knowledge of beer brands and slogans, alcohol beliefs, intentions to drink as adults, perceived peer and parental drinking and approval of drinking, and finally demographics and background. All the data were entered into a complex structural equations model and analyzed.

The study has all the hallmarks of a quasi-experimental investigation and all of the concomitant limitations. Chief among these is the cross-sectional nature of the survey approach and hence the fact that all results are correlational and not causal, a point the authors took pains to identify. And yet a presumed ordering of effects was assumed "consistent with previous research and theory" (p. 256). As a consequence, "unidirectional effects from awareness of beer advertising to beliefs and knowledge and from beliefs to intentions" (p. 256) was assumed and operationalized in the model. One could, of course, argue about the chosen priority of effects since there are equally compelling reasons to suggest that intentions to drink cause differential attention to ads as well as knowledge of brand imagery and slogans.

Endless circular arguments concerning which came first—ads or intentions aside—the results of the study were consistent with others that have used surveys and quasi-experimental methods to investigate advertising and alcohol use. The authors note that advertising awareness indirectly affected intentions to drink through positive beliefs about alcohol. When the paths are linked and the combined probability of advertising first affecting positive beliefs and subsequently intentions to drink is calculated, we find that advertising explains 2.26% of the variance in drinking intentions. This figure is right in the middle of the range, .2 to 4.0% reported in other quasi-experimental studies, for the variance in alcohol consumption explained by advertising exposure (see Fisher, 1993, Table 6.4).

Another survey study addressed the use of warning labels and advertising in prevention efforts. A survey of 1,211 twelfth-graders (MacKinnon et al., 1993) examined government mandated warning labels on alcoholic beverage containers. The researchers found that one year after the warning label law went into effect there were significant increases in awareness of the labels and knowledge of some risks, but there was no association between label awareness and alcohol use or beliefs about risks given in the warning. These findings are consistent with others (Engs, 1989; Mayer et al., 1991; Scammon et al., 1991) that found that product warning labels generally and labels on alcoholic beverage containers specifically had little impact on consumer behavior.

Finally, Lipsitz et al. (1993) conducted an experiment of alcohol expectancies and exposure to television beer commercials. The 92 fifth-graders included in the study were divided into three treatment groups. Each group viewed 40 commercials. For one group 5 of the 40 were beer ads, a second group saw five soft-drink ads instead of beer commercials, and the last treatment consisted of five beer ads and two anti-drinking messages. The study was then repeated with a sample of 74 eighth-graders.

Following both administrations, the investigators found that neither exposure to beer advertisements nor anti-drinking messages had a significant effect on alcohol expectancies. Interpreting their findings in the light of past research the author's concluded:

> Another possible explanation, of course, is that alcohol advertising simply does not affect alcohol expectancies. Perhaps the null findings obtained here mirror a reality of television ads having no impact or relatively minimal impact on youngsters' feelings about alcohol. To date, there is no strong evidence to the contrary; as stated earlier, survey studies have found only small correlations with ambiguous interpretations, and experimental studies have found no results or results that were nonrobust. (Lipsitz et al., 1993, p. 448)

But having come this far the investigators found it impossible to accept their own findings and the preponderance of evidence that supported their conclusions. Shying away from the implications of their results, the authors continued

> nevertheless, the notion of no relationship between alcohol advertising and children's alcohol attitudes seems implausible, as so many theories would predict otherwise. Also, as alcohol ads are some of the most expensive and sophisticated ads on television, it is hard to believe that manufacturers do not think they create positive expectancies in youthful viewers. More research, employing alternative methodologies, is clearly called for. As mentioned previously, the possibility of bans on alcohol commercials continues to be discussed. Theoretically, a ban makes sense; empirically, it cannot be justified. (Lipsitz et al., 1993, p. 448)

The authors' retention of belief that advertising must after all affect drinking behavior puts an interesting twist on the philosophy of science, when theory is used to deny empirical findings rather than experimental results used to disprove theories.

The research published in the last two years does not therefore cause us to alter any of the conclusions drawn when the literature was reviewed in a comprehensive fashion earlier. Quite the contrary, newly published results are entirely consistent with the body of evidence that has been previously reported in scientific journals. But despite the accumulated learning of scores of studies across a wide range of disciplines there remains a persistent reluctance in the research community to accept the findings at face value. A tendency exists to tenaciously hold on to theories and conceptual models in spite of their inability to predict behavior. And when all else fails there is always the comforting argument that advertising spending by manufacturers is *prima facie* evidence that advertising does indeed promote increased drinking.

STUDY DESIGN

Although the literature review indicates that advertising has little impact on total alcohol consumption and therefore by implication a minor role, if any, in alcohol-related health and social problems, it is important to note that the conclusion is drawn based on a compilation of evidence most of which addressed discrete points along the causal continuum. Studies that span the full process from exposure to behavior to negative consequences are exceedingly rare. And even these have methodology limitations that create ambiguity in the results.

Content analyses and experiments by their very nature are not equipped to evaluate the full chain of effects but rather are confined to specific points. Quasi-experimental research can look at the full range of behaviors, but, only a handful of studies have done so. Moreover, the point-in-time survey method forces investigators to project a causal flow on what are ultimately only correlational or relational findings. Studies that use time series methods, econometric studies of demand, and evaluations of changes in permissible advertising may be the best suited methodologically to address the full behavioral chain, but to date, investigators have not taken full advantage of the opportunity.

Econometricians, for instance, are typically only concerned with estimating elasticities, in other words the change in consumption that accompanies changes in prices, income, or advertising. As a group, econometricians, who are engaged in estimating demand for alcohol products, have been singularly uninterested in quantifying the public health consequences of any observed consumption changes, a truly unfortunate circumstance given their analyses tend to be the most sophisticated and their method among the best suited to the pursuit.

Evaluations of advertising policy changes also have tended to eschew the public health dimension again focusing almost exclusively on consumption. Additionally, changes in advertising are measured in a gross and rudimentary way, as a simple binary variable 0 before the change and 1 after. This "intervention effect" is not quantified in terms of actual changes in media exposure such as number of ads shown, changes in media expenditures or gross rating points (GRPs), that is, impressions. As noted earlier, this is an especially worrisome oversight given the increasing globalization of the media environment and advertising spillover from unaffected areas.

In the present study we have attempted to retain the best of the econometric tradition while extending its application to examine negative consequences that could be associated with increased consumption. To be specific, we will examine alcohol consumption in the United States over four decades from 1950–1990. Trends in consumption will be related to factors that are believed to influence demand, price, income, advertising, and demography in a time series framework. From this analysis we will attempt to determine what role advertising might play in promoting alcohol consumption. Subsequently, we will relate consumption to mortality rates for alcohol-related disease such as cirrhosis of the liver or alcoholic psychosis. This analysis will be used to determine the indirect effect, through consumption, of advertising on mortality rates and to compare the impact of advertising with that of other factors such as price.

The literature review provides further guidance on the construction of the study design. Initially, econometric work (e.g., Weinberg, 1984) has shown that some demand for some alcohol products in the United States is sensitive to demographic shifts. We have, as a consequence, included an indicator of the heavy drinking segment of the population. Second, econometric studies outside of North America have shown convincingly that consumption of alcoholic beverages is a system of manifest consumer choices in which various beverage classes substitute for one another. We have adopted the same approach by considering all three beverage categories as well as total consumption in a unified analytic context. Third, we have made explicit the theoretical underpinnings of the causal chain in the ordering of effects. Thus, we will look for advertising to affect mortality only as it is mediated through total consumption as predicted by the single distribution theory. And finally, we intend to test the entire range of behavior from exposure to consumption to adverse outcomes.

A schematic version of the study design is given in Figure 1.3. We will consider five types of demand predictors, three that are common to all beverage categories, demographic, income and trend, and two that are specific to a single beverage class, price and advertising. We will examine the influence of these factors on the categories of alcohol products individually and then as required by the single distribution theory on total consumption. Last, again as stipulated by the single distribution theory, total consumption will be related to mortality rates. The impact of any given demand predicator, like advertising, on mortality can then be calculated as it progresses through the chain of causality.

We believe our conceptual model and analytic approach is unique and will extend beyond past efforts for several reasons:

Figure 1.3
Conceptual Model and Study Design

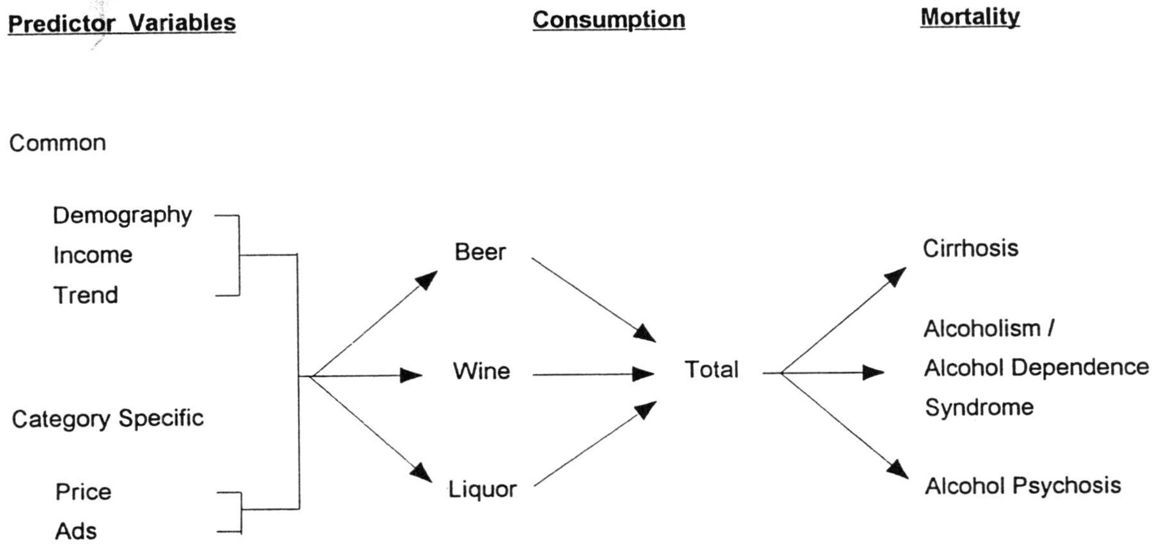

Predictor Variables	**Consumption**	**Mortality**

Common

Demography
Income
Trend

Category Specific

Price
Ads

Beer

Wine

Liquor

Total

Cirrhosis

Alcoholism /
Alcohol Dependence
Syndrome

Alcohol Psychosis

1. *Predictor Variables*: Demography is considered as well as strictly economic variables.

2. *Systemwide*: All alcohol consumption is considered, at the category level and in total.

3. *Theoretical Accuracy*: Effects will be sought as predicted by the single distribution theory as a function of changes in total consumption.

4. *Causal Chain*: The full range of behavioral consequences, consumption and mortality, will be investigated in a single analytic context.

And last, true to the scientific method and the previously conducted literature review we will state the purpose of the investigation in null form. We will test the hypothesis: Advertising has no effect on total consumption of alcohol or rates of mortality from alcohol-related disease.

ORGANIZATION OF THE TEXT

The content of the following chapter parallels the progression of effects given in Figure 1.3. Initially, in Chapter 2, we will define and describe the variables, both predictor and outcome, that will be used in the models of alcohol consumption. For each conceptual variable, like supply or alternately income, we will describe how the variable is operationalized and measured. The source of the data is provided as is a discussion of any limitations of the measurement or transformations that have been applied to the data. Chapter 2 then presents a descriptive summary of the data including distributional statistics in tabular form and trends over time in graphic mode. Implications for consumption and share of consumption are also given.

Chapter 3 presents the results of the first of two demand analyses. In this case, raw or equivalently untransformed data are used to estimate demand for alcohol and hence in many respects these analyses quantify the gross trends charted in Chapter 2. Two demand models are given; the first for consumption of the three alcoholic beverage categories and the second for share of total consumption. Next we examine systemwide effects in which total consumption is combined with consumption of the three beverage types and shares of consumption by means of factor analyses and regressions on the predictor variables. The chapter concludes with the presentation of results of corroborative analyses, one set involving the use of alternative specifications for advertising in the demand models and the second an investigation of time series relationships, leads and lags, between advertising and alcohol consumption.

Chapter 4 repeats the analyses given in Chapter 3 but does so after an important transformation has been made on the data. Specifically, the raw data have been differenced such that the analyses concentrate on change over time. The data values for both predictor and consumption variables become the changes from one year to the next. After the data are transformed we again estimate demand for consumption and share of consumption. Change in total consumption is considered with another set of factor analytic regressions. As before, different advertising specifications are evaluated and the time series structure is investigated.

Chapter 5 takes up the issue of mortality. We will focus the discussion on three diseases that are clearly related to consumption of alcohol—cirrhosis of the liver with alcohol specified, alcoholism or alcohol dependence syndrome, and alcoholic psychosis—and therefore represent the most likely causes of death for which a link to consumption and advertising might be seen. We will begin by describing the trends in mortality rates for these diseases over the 40-year study period. Next, total consumption will be related to mortality contemporaneously and over time. The third step is to model advertising and other effects, for example, price, through consumption to mortality as shown in Figure 1.3. The final analysis given in Chapter 5 attempts to simulate how mortality rates and numbers of deaths might be affected if advertising or prices changed by a specified amount.

The results of all the analyses are assembled and interpreted in Chapter 6. The major findings of the study regarding trends over time, category consumption, share of consumption, total consumption, and effects on mortality are recapitulated. Additionally, we will attempt to draw together the collective meaning of the findings into a series of conclusions regarding the role advertising plays in alcohol consumption and death from alcohol-related disease that seem warranted from the data. The ultimate goal will be to determine if the null hypothesis should be accepted or rejected. Finally, we will offer some suggestions for the future research in the area.

One final note on terminology before we begin with the description of the data. Throughout this text a number of terms are used interchangeably to relieve the tedium of the discussion. Alcohol consumption is, as an example, referred to equivalently as alcohol demand; variables that are thought to influence consumption are called demand determinants, predictors, and independent variables; while variables that are thought to be influenced are termed outcome or dependent variables as well as demand or consumption. Three beverage categories are considered in the analysis: beer or malt products, wine, and liquor or distilled products. Categories are also called beverage types or classes.

Most importantly, alcohol consumption in our study has a very specific meaning. It is the consumption of pure alcohol, known alternately as raw or absolute alcohol. The various beverage categories differ with respect to their content of pure alcohol, beer 4.5%, wine 12.9%, and liquor 41.4% (Williams et al., 1993), and total consumption figures have been factored to obtain the amount of pure or 100% alcohol that is consumed by drinking products in each category. The primary advantages of this representation are that all drinking regardless of category can be combined to obtain a total alcohol consumption figure as required by the single distribution theory and volumetric data over time can be directly compared across categories to yield accurate share of consumption figures. In the text then we refer to raw, absolute, or simply alcohol consumption and note that it is sourced from drinking products in a particular category.

Chapter 2

Data Description

In many respects the statistical analyses that are reported in later chapters quantify the basic trends and relationships that are present in the data, interrelated patterns that are often visually apparent when the data are tabulated and displayed in simple form. The numerical context within which the more sophisticated analyses will be conducted and interpreted is the subject of this chapter. Of particular interest will be alcohol consumption and its determinants. Mortality from alcohol-related disease will be considered in depth in Chapter 5.

In this chapter we will look initially at how conceptual demand determinants such as income, price, or demography will be operationalized. That is, how the concepts will be measured, how the predictor variables will be defined. We will also note the source of each variable, the limitations, if any, in measurement, and describe any standardization or adjustments that have been made. The outcome variables, consumption and share of consumption, will be treated in a like manner. After the data set has been defined we will display the data in numerical and graphical form. The objective will be to point out gross historical trends in economic conditions and demography that will, in turn, provide a basis for interpretation when the demand models are built and results are reported.

DATA DEFINITIONS

The basic demand models that will be reported in Chapters 3 and 4 consist of economic factors (supply and demand), demography, advertising, and a linear trend component as well as the outcome variables consumption and share of consumption. The conceptual demand determinants, in turn, were broken down into five categories of variables including: beverage price (supply), income (demand), population, beverage advertising, and year. Each of the variables used in the demand models, predictor and outcome, are described below.

Price

Actual prices were not available for the three beverage categories. Instead, the Consumer Price Index for each beverage type was obtained from the Bureau of Labor Statistics. These data were based on the U.S. city average of all urban consumers and were standardized such that the average index of the years 1982–1984 was 100. Price indices were available for beer and liquor for 38 years, 1953–1990, but were only available for the period 1964–1990 for wine. Lack of price data limited the range over which wine demand could be studied to 27 years, therefore.

Price indices increase over time as a function of macroeconomic effects such as inflation. Moreover, for purposes of the demand models the price index of any given beverage type is less significant than whether or not alcoholic beverages have gotten less or more expensive relative to some standard. For this reason, the price index of each beverage class was divided by the Consumer Price Index (CPI) for all items. The resulting measure of relative price for the three beverage types was used in the demand models and is indicated by the mnemonic Price.

Income

Disposable personal income was used as an indictor of demand and was obtained from the Bureau of Economic Analysis, Survey of Current Business. These data were expressed per capita (15 years or older) and were deflated to 1982 dollars to correspond to the price indices. Thus, deflated (1982 dollars), per capita (15 years or older) disposable personal income was used as the measure of demand in the context of supply and demand of economic theory and is referred to as Income in tables and charts.

Population

A number of studies (Levy and Sheflin, 1985; Norman, 1975; Orenstein and Levy, 1983; Weinberg, 1984) have found that demography affects alcohol consumption, specifically, demand for malt beverages. Of particular importance in this regard is the young adult population, loosely defined as those of legal drinking age through age 35. This segment of the population exhibits two strong predilections that critically impact demand for alcohol products: the heaviest average consumption and distinct product preferences. For purposes of this study the young adult population was defined to be persons between the ages of 20 and 34 years old. Yearly figures for the young adult population were expressed in millions and included in the demand models as simple counts. Hence, the number of millions of persons between the ages of 20 and 34 years old was used as the demographic indicator and is referred to as Population in tables and graphs.

Demographic statistics affect the analysis in another crucial fashion, through the calculation of rates. In all cases, rates are calculated on an adult per capita basis where adult is defined to be persons 15 years or older in the United States. All population figures were drawn from the U.S. Department of Commerce, Bureau of the Census, Current Population Reports, Estimates of the Resident Population of the United States, By Age, Sex, and Race. These reports estimate the resident population of the United States, including Alaska and Hawaii and armed forces stationed in the United States. We have chosen to eliminate estimates of armed forces stationed overseas from the population figures since we believed these individuals would not contribute substantially to alcohol consumption figures. Hence, only residents of the United States and armed forces personnel stationed in the United States were included in the total adult population figures used to calculate rates and in the estimates of the young adult population segment.

Trend

To remove linear trends in the raw data and quadratic effects in the first difference models, the year to which data pertain was included in all demand analyses and is denoted Year in the illustrations.

Advertising—Magazines

Two types of advertising data were available for the study. The first, obtained from the Publishers Information Bureau, Leading National Advertisers (LNA) reports, deals specifically with on-page advertising in major consumer magazines. These data were available for all three beverage categories from 1950–1990 and were expressed as either the number of pages or total spending. Magazine spending, denoted Magazine Ad $, was used in the demand models as the primary measure of advertising for each beverage category. As always magazine advertising spending was deflated to 1982 dollars to make the series comparable with other data expressed in dollars. The yearly number of magazine advertising pages by category, Magazine Pages, was used as a secondary indicator of advertising to corroborate any observed effects.

Using magazine spending as a measure of total advertising is not without drawbacks. There is initially the minor methodological concern that the consumer magazines in which pages were counted and advertising dollars calculated changed from year to year. Roughly 100 magazines having the largest circulation and representing a wide array of categories[1] were monitored each year, the vast majority of which remained constant over time and appeared in every sample. Nevertheless, each year a small number of magazines were dropped or added to the sample, typically ± 5 titles. Although this creates some year-to-year variability in the base on which measurements were taken, it was not deemed to be a serious problem since the overwhelming position of the sample remained the same each year. Further, each beverage group was measured in the same set of magazines each year, and hence any error introduced could be expected to be proportional for each class of beverage.

Of much greater concern is the fact that magazines represent a very different media opportunity for marketers of the three beverage categories. Liquor advertising is prohibited in many media, particularly broadcast, and hence a disproportionately large share of liquor advertising budgets are spent in print, specifically magazines. Conversely, with a wider set of options in which to expend funds, magazine advertising tends to represent a relatively minor share of the total advertising budget for beer and wine. This problem would not compromise the demand models if magazine advertising represented a constant share of total advertising expenditures for each beverage type. Thus, even though the absolute relationship between advertising and consumption might be understated in absolute dollars, the strength and direction of the relationship (i.e., the regression coefficient) would accurately reflect the overall effect. As we will see in a moment, this assumption is tenuous at best.

Advertising—All Media

Advertising spending in a full range of media has been tracked since 1970 and these data were made available by Competitive Media Research. In particular, six major media were monitored throughout the entire period including: network television, spot television, network radio, outdoor (billboards), newspaper supplements, and, of course, magazines. Four other media were added to the list during the study period, specifically, cable television, 1984–1990; newspapers, 1988–1990; syndicated television, 1988–1990; and spot radio, 1990.

From these data we calculated two indicators of alcoholic beverage category advertising spending. The first, Total 6 Media, is the sum of advertising spending for a beverage category such as beer across the six media that were monitored for the full 1970–1990 period. The second indicator is Total Media and is simply the sum of all the advertising for a category in all the media measured in that year, that is, six media from 1970–1983, seven from 1984–1987, nine from 1988–1989, and ten in 1990. All advertising spending figures were deflated to 1982 dollars.

Clearly Total 6 Media and Total Media provide the best estimates of advertising expenditures for each beverage category. As an example, category spending for beer products in 1990 was $648.1 million (undeflated) of which $30.1 million or 4.6% was spent in magazines. Comparable figures for wine products were $97.2 million total and $15.3 million or 15.7% in magazines, and for the liquor category $280.2 million total of which the lion's share $228.2 million or 81.4% was in magazines.

Taking up the issue mentioned earlier, the difference in proportional advertising spending in magazines by category would not in its own right be a fatal problem if the amount of magazine spending were to represent a fairly constant fraction of total advertising expenditures for each category. As noted before, under these conditions, the regression coefficients for advertising in the demand models would be directionally accurate, tests of significance would be valid and the numerical value of the coefficient would be proportional to the "true" advertising effect. To investigate whether the assumption of constant proportionality was reasonable we plotted magazine spending as a fraction of total advertising for the period 1970–1990 (Figure 2.1).

It can be seen from the graph that magazine spending does represent a fairly regular component of total advertising expenditures for the three beverage types. For instance, magazine spending for liquor products ranges from 70 to 80% of total spending. For wine products like figures are 10 to 30% and for beer 5 to 10%. The proportions are deceptively stable in some respects however. Although the percentages appear quite constant there is nonetheless relatively big swings from year to year. More importantly, the swings tend to be biggest for the product categories whose spending is least likely to be accurately represented by magazine spending. As a result, a variation of 10 to 30% for wine is, in fact, a range of 200% over the base levels, whereas for beer a 5 to 10% swing is 100% variability. On closer inspection it seems then that the assumption of constant proportionality cannot be safely made.

Ultimately, we were presented with a dilemma: whether to use the most accurate quantification of category advertising spending but cut the study period in half or to maintain the length of the time series investigated by using an imperfect advertising measurement. We opted for the latter strategy believing the analysis was compromised least by using a less than satisfactory advertising specification. A longer time series was deemed critical to the analysis so that short-term trends would not produce misleading or biased results.

Although we have made Magazine Ad $ the primary specification of advertising in the analysis, we repeated the analyses and built demand models for every advertising definition. In the text that follows, the discussion will be oriented primarily around the results for the Magazine Ad $ specification. We will also report and interpret the results for the other specifications to determine if they corroborate or contradict the findings for Magazine Ad $. Consequently, every demand model, for raw data and first differences, testing the relationship between advertising and consumption or share of consumption was constructed four times for each advertising specification.

Alcohol Consumption

The principal outcome measures in the demand models were per capita adult alcohol consumption by beverage type and in total and share of total consumption for the beverage classes. Per capita alcohol consumption statistics were

Figure 2.1
Magazine Spending as a Percentage of Total Advertising Spending

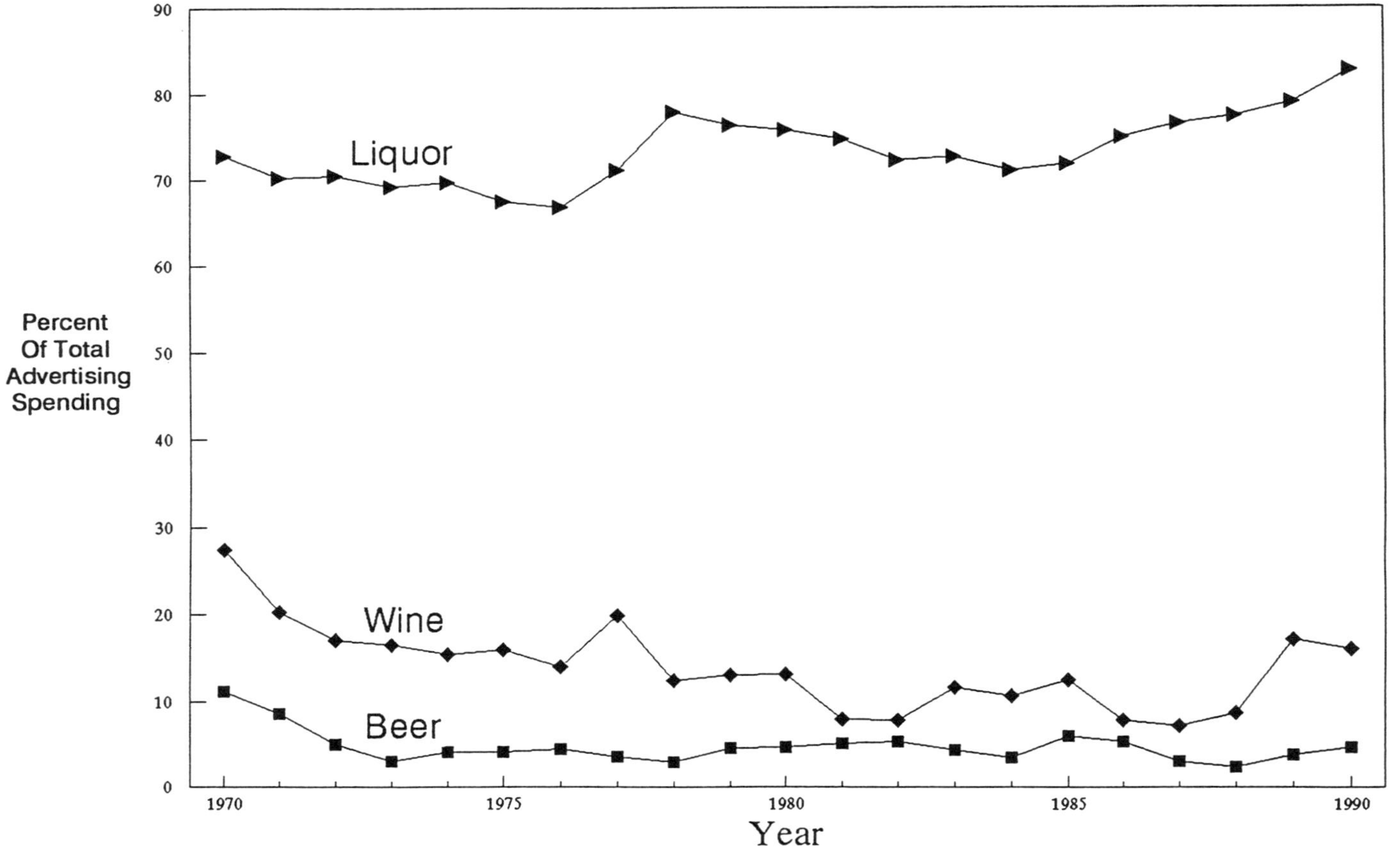

obtained from the National Institute of Alcohol Abuse and Alcoholism, Division of Biometry and Epidemiology, Surveillance Report #27 (Williams et al., 1993). All figures for the three alcoholic beverage categories and total consumption were expressed as gallons of absolute alcohol per adult per year.

Consumption figures were available for the full study period but were not measured consistently throughout. From 1940–1969 per capita estimates were based on persons 15 years or older, while from 1970–1990 the population of individuals 14 years or older was used as the base for per capita calculations. To correct for the change in methodology and to make the consumption series consistent with other per capita figures in the study, 1970–1990 statistics were adjusted for the number of 14-year-olds in the population and reexpressed as per capita consumption for persons 15 years or older.

DATA DESCRIPTION

The descriptive statistics for the predictor variables, including the mean, standard deviation, low and high values, and the number of years for which data were available is given in Table 2.1. With respect to population, the young adult segment, aged 20- to 34-years-old, averaged slightly over 46 million persons for the duration of the study. Young adults represented just under a quarter of the entire population, 22.4%, on average over the four decades studied.

These averages tend to obscure one of the major social trends that is present in the data set, however, namely the coming of age of the post–World War II baby boom. This stunning trend is shown quite vividly in Figure 2.2. In 1950 the young adult population was roughly 34 million individuals and stayed at that level until 1965. The 20- to 34-year-old segment then grew dramatically nearly doubling in size and reaching a peak of 63.1 million persons by 1985. On a percentage basis, the segment grew from 18.3% of the population to 26.5%.

The implications of this demographic wave for our research is straightforward. First, young adults tend to be the heaviest consumers of alcoholic beverage products. We might expect a commensurate increase in per capita consumption of total alcohol as a consequence. Second, younger drinkers evidence distinct beverage preferences, favoring beer and to a lesser degree wine over distilled beverage products. We would expect to see a greater percentage of total alcohol consumption sourced from beer products over time and a shift in share of consumption to malt products from liquor ones.

Another equally dramatic dynamic operating involves the accumulation of wealth on the part of the average American. At the start of the study period the entire personal disposable income for the country was $208 billion. Forty years later it had grown 20 times to $4 trillion. Even when we express these figures on a per capita basis and adjust for inflation the change in affluence is still staggering. As can be seen in Figure 2.3 in 1950 the average adult American had just under eight thousand dollars, $7,869.60 to be exact, of disposable income. Forty years later individual personal disposable income had doubled in

Table 2.1
Descriptive Statistics for Predictor Variables

Predictor Variables	Mean	Standard Deviation	Low	High	Years
Population 20–34 (000,000)	46.25	11.96	33.60	63.12	41
% Total Population	22.37	2.96	18.26	26.50	41
Income ($000)	12.11	2.43	7.77	15.99	41
Price Index Beer (/CPI)	1.23	.19	.95	1.50	41
Wine (/CPI)	1.13	.16	.87	1.34	41
Liquor (/CPI)	1.61	.49	.95	2.19	41
Magazine Ad $ Beer ($000,000)	21.80	7.30	6.08	33.71	41
Wine ($000,000)	13.39	4.33	5.60	21.16	41
Liquor ($000,000)	166.07	52.16	80.54	283.38	41
Magazine Pages Beer	435.49	136.63	134.60	823.60	41
Wine	537.14	110.16	354.20	864.49	41
Liquor	4,281.59	1,503.98	2,494.18	8,312.66	41

Figure 2.2
Young Adult Population, Ages 20–34

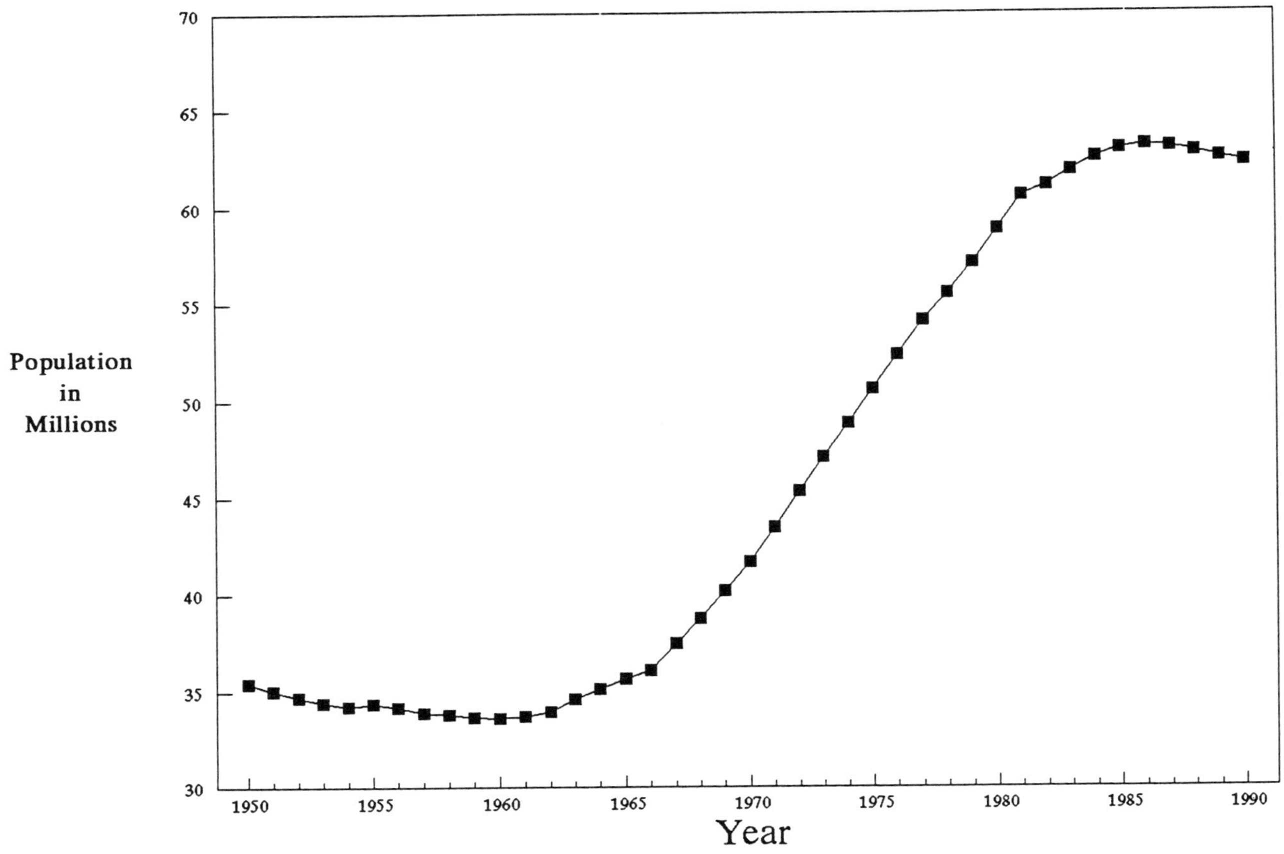

Population
in
Millions

Year

Figure 2.3
Deflated Personal Disposable Income per Capita

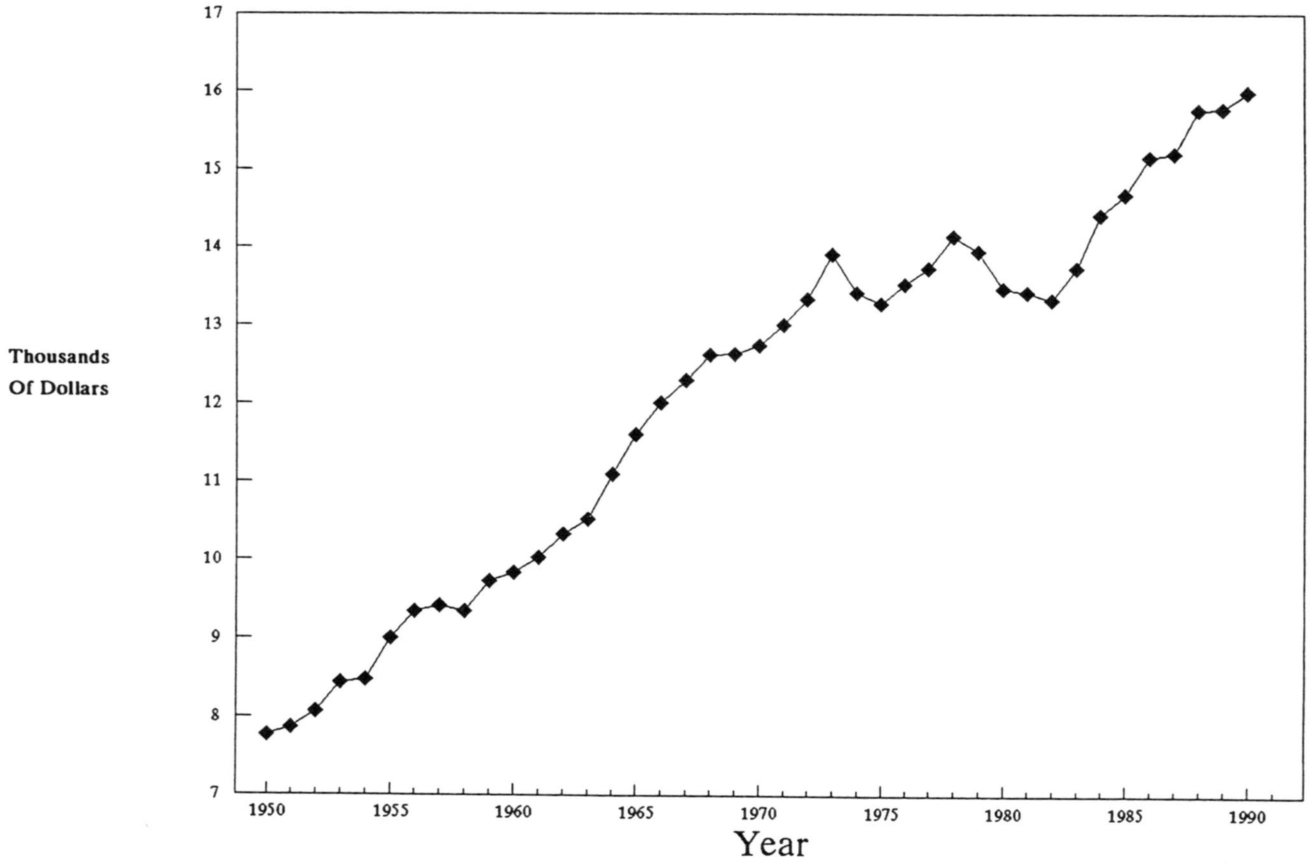

Thousands
Of Dollars

Year

real terms to $15,998.70. Hence, every person in the United States 15 years or older had nearly $16,000 (in 1982 terms) of disposable income in 1990.

Again, the implications for alcohol consumption should be direct and promote increased alcohol consumption. A number of econometricians, especially in the United Kingdom (Clements and Selvanathan, 1988; Duffy, 1987, 1989, 1990; Selvanathan, 1989), have found that consumers spend a fairly constant percentage, 6 to 8%, of their annual household budgets on alcohol products. Interestingly, the percentage of household budget or alternately personal disposable income spent on alcohol products was found to be quite stable cross-culturally. What varied from one country to the next was the mix of products purchased. As an example while Britons and Australians each spent between 6 and 8% of disposable income on alcohol products, Australians spent a greater share on beer products while the English favored distilled spirits.

If we suppose that Americans follow this pattern and spend a relatively constant amount on alcoholic beverages and that this percentage of personal disposable income has remained stable over time, then Americans would have twice as much to spend on alcohol products just as a function of the growing affluence of the public over time. Quite simply, Americans could spend twice as much without modifying their traditional mix of household purchases. We might reasonably expect the accumulation of personal wealth to stimulate increased consumption, therefore.

Another effect should also be consequent of the growth in disposable income. In particular, expensive alcohol products, notably liquor, should come within reach of more consumers. We might forecast then a movement in share away from beer toward more expensive wines and distilled spirits. Clearly, this share shift pressure would tend to counteract or be offset by the presumed impact of the surge in the young adult population.

Price, or alternatively, supply, is the second economic variable included in the demand model, and here again, we see evidence of major structural changes in the country that should have significant ramifications for alcohol consumption. In this case, we have three measures of price, one for each beverage type, and these are expressed relative to the Consumer Price Index for all consumer products. To illustrate, the mean value for beer products over the last four decades was 122.6; that is, beer prices averaged 22.6% above all consumer products over the period. Similarly, wine prices were 13.5% and liquor 61.3% above the norm. So on average alcohol products were relatively expensive over time and liquor products were the most expensive when compared with all consumer products.

But again the averages misrepresent the profound changes that have taken place since 1950. There has been a precipitous decline in the relative prices of all alcoholic beverage classes but especially liquor (Figure 2.4). In 1953 liquor products were over two times the CPI, 218.7; by 1990 they had fallen to just under the CPI, 95.5. It is worth restating these numbers. At the start of the study period, liquor products were 118.7% above the CPI for all consumer products

Figure 2.4
Alcohol Price Index Relative to CPI

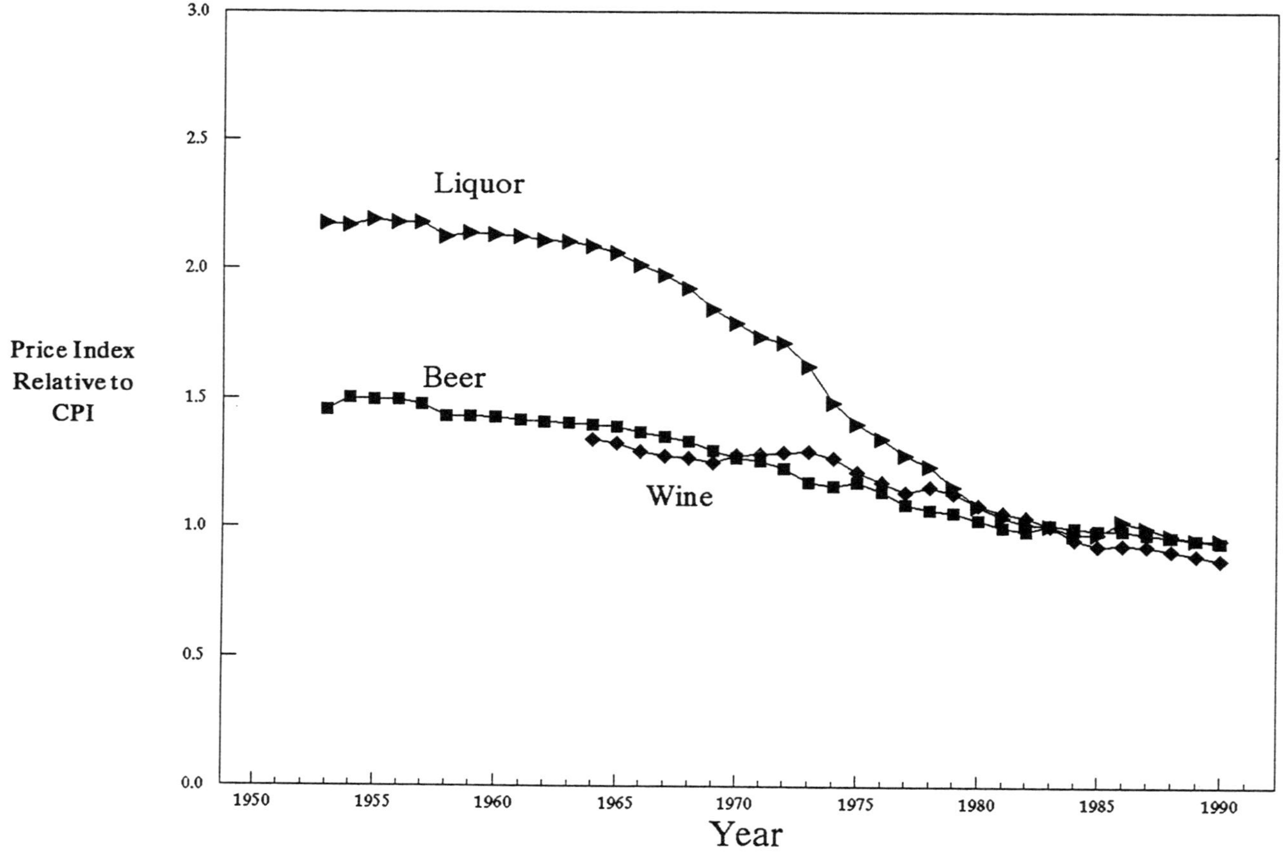

whereas by 1990 they were 4.5% below the CPI. Liquor fell 60% on a relative basis, or stated differently it was 40% as expensive to buy liquor products at the end of the period than at the start.

Beer and wine products also became relatively less expensive but the change was far less dramatic. Beer declined from 150.2 or 50.2% above the CPI in 1953 to 94.6 or 5.4% below the CPI by 1990. Wine price indices were only available from 1964 forward but nonetheless over this time frame relative prices fell by more than fifty percent. Wine prices were 34.2% higher than the CPI in 1964 but 12.5% below in 1990. The trend is clear-cut for all beverage classes, alcoholic products have become less expensive on a relative basis over time.

Again the likely impact of falling relative prices on alcohol consumption should be to stimulate increased consumption. Very simply alcohol products have become less expensive since World War II and therefore within reach of more consumers. More importantly, prices have fallen relative to other consumer products and presumably nonalcoholic beverage substitutes. The price barrier to drinking an alcoholic beverage instead of a nonalcoholic alternative lowered over time and we might expect a consequent increase in alcohol consumption.

The last predictor variables included in the demand models were the indicators of advertising for the three alcoholic beverage categories. As we review the media statistics it is clear that there has been an explosive growth in advertising over the 40 years studied and this growth takes two forms: (1) in the number of media options available to manufacturers to reach and persuade consumers and (2) in the growth of real advertising spending over the study period. With respect to the first trend, we have already noted that it was possible to track only one medium, magazine advertising, for the entire study period. By 1990 there were ten different media tracked routinely and of these four had emerged as important advertising options only in the last five years. Given the advent of an increased use of direct marketing, addressable consumer databases, 500-channel television, interactive media, and on-line cyberspace services, it is unlikely that the burgeoning growth in media options will slacken anytime soon. Quite the contrary, it seems likely that more opportunities will be found to reach consumers and target messages more precisely to their projected interests, wants, and needs.

The second major trend in advertising is the increase in real advertising spending for alcohol products. This trend is boldly evident if we look again at the range of deflated magazine advertising spending figures in Table 2.1. Note that magazine advertising spending for beer products had a low value of $6 million but grew five times reaching a high of nearly $34 million. Wine spending increased four times from a low of $5.6 million to a high of $21.2 million, while spending for liquor products increased three and a half times, $80.5 million at the lowest to $283.4 million at the highest. The number of pages committed to advertising for the three beverage types tells a similar story. Beer pages increase by a factor of six, wine pages doubled, and the number of magazine pages devoted to liquor advertising tripled.

The tremendous growth in media spending for alcohol products is not confined solely to magazine advertising. Table 2.2 shows the media spending for beer, wine and liquor in Total 6 Media and Total Media from 1970 to 1990. For Total 6 Media beer advertising averaged $386.5 million over the 21-year period. However, as shown in Figure 2.5, spending for beer products was at its lowest in real terms at the start of the period totaling $181.4 million a year. Nineteen years later in 1988 advertising spending more than tripled, exceeding $600 million, $604.8 million to be exact. The growth in spending for wine products was even larger on a percentage basis, increasing three and one half times from $58.7 million a year in 1970 to $209.3 million in the late 1980s. Advertising spending for liquor products followed a somewhat different course. Spending in Total 6 Media merely doubled from $188.5 million to $371.1 million, and further peak spending levels were reached in the early 1980s.

If we consider the entire advertising spending for the alcoholic beverage segment, Total Media in Table 2.2, we can see that from 1970 to 1990 the average annual advertising spending in all media was $791 million. At the lowest point in 1970, the combined spending was $446.4 million. By the late 1980s total advertising spending on all alcohol products tripled in real terms to just under one and a quarter billion dollars, $1,225.7 million. It is clear then that over time manufacturers expended significantly more of their corporate resources advertising their products. Further the increase is real growth and not simply a function of inflation. The reasons for the greater reliance on advertising are uncertain. It could be a function of a proliferation in new products or line extensions (e.g., lite beers, wine coolers) all of which require incremental advertising expenditures. It might also signal the maturing of the marketplace and a consequent increase in competition among products. Manufacturers might be forced to increase advertising spending, therefore, to maintain their historical market share.

It is also difficult to predict how the growth in media options and advertising spending might affect total consumption. On the surface it would seem reasonable to think that advertising would act as a stimulant to consumption. There is little doubt that manufacturers have made great efforts to reach and persuade consumers. But the question remains—persuade them to do what? If the appeal is tied to individual brands we might expect significant share shifts between products in a category but little between categories and perhaps even less to alcoholic beverages from nonalcoholic alternatives.

Of course, shifting consumption to alcoholic beverages from nonalcoholic substitutes is not the only way advertising could affect total consumption. It could reinforce drinking thereby shortening the time between drinking occasions or by making it more likely that an alcoholic beverage would be selected in the future. It might also serve to promote increased consumption at every drinking occasion and hence an alcoholic beverage would not necessarily need to be substituted for a nonalcoholic one at a particular time. Instead, when alcoholic beverages are consumed the average amount drunk per occasion increases. Our data will not allow us to examine these individual and occasion-based dynamics.

Table 2.2
Descriptive Statistics for Alternative Media Specifications

Annual Media Spending ($000,000)		Mean	Standard Deviation	Low	High	Years
Total 6 Media	Beer	386.50	141.12	181.37	604.77	21
	Wine	120.81	43.32	58.71	209.27	21
	Liquor	265.09	50.60	188.45	371.09	21
Total Media	Beer	401.21	154.88	181.37	639.41	21
	Wine	123.58	42.91	67.83	215.22	21
	Liquor	266.17	49.24	197.23	371.09	21

Figure 2.5
Deflated Total Media Spending

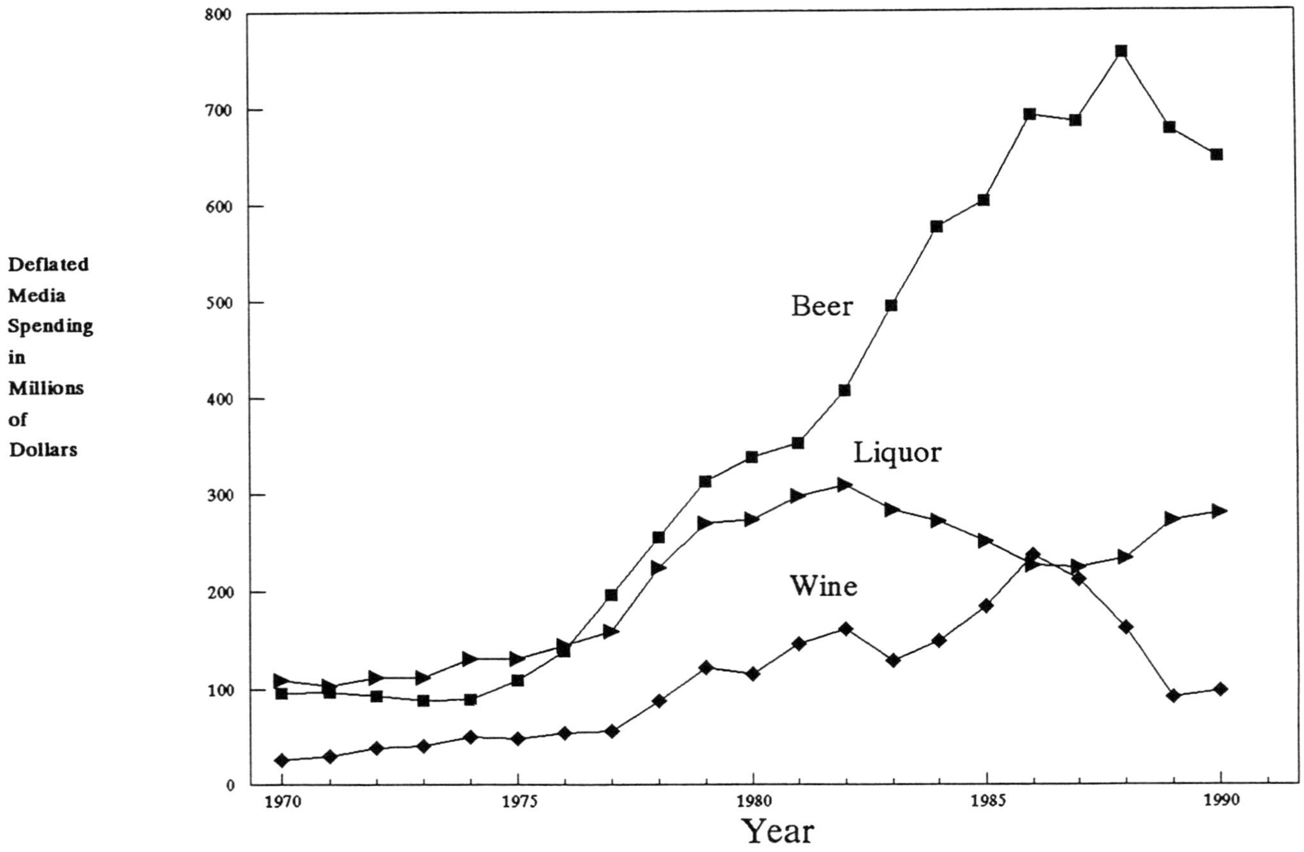

Deflated
Media
Spending
in
Millions
of
Dollars

Beer

Liquor

Wine

Year

If they are operative to any meaningful degree, total consumption will be measurably affected and we will be forced to look for the effects of advertising on an aggregate level, that is, how it affects total consumption.

Before we conclude our discussion of advertising, there is one other comparison that provides some insight into trends over time. Figure 2.6 shows the share of Total Media spending by beverage category from 1970 to 1990. Displaying media spending in this fashion, what media professionals call share of voice, or SOV, reveals how the relative spending of each beverage category has changed over the period. At the beginning of the 1970s beer and liquor spending was comparable with shares just over 40% with liquor the slightly higher of the two. Wine share of voice was roughly 10% and remained at this approximate level for the next two decades. Larger shifts were apparent for beer and liquor spending. Share of voice for beer products outstripped that for the liquor category in 1976 and continued to climb at the expense of liquor share of voice for the next 15 years. By the later 1980s beer share of voice was more than triple that for liquor, 60% versus 20%.

Based on these figures, if advertising influences category as well as brand shares, we might expect to find that beer share of total consumption increases over time. Furthermore, this increase in share for beer products would be gained almost exclusively from liquor consumption. Other factors such as the coincident growth of the 20- to 34-year segment of the population should abet and accelerate this structural shift. Wine share meanwhile might be expected, based on advertising spending patterns alone, to remain fairly constant.

To this point we have examined the gross trends in the variables that are thought to influence alcohol consumption. We have additionally forecast what we believe the impact on consumption and share of consumption would be for each of the trends. Before moving on to what in fact happened to consumption and share of consumption over the four decades studied it is worth reviewing quickly the basic trends in the data and their presumed impact on alcohol consumption.

First, there was a dramatic increase in the young adult population of the country as the post–World War II baby boom came of age and became legal drinkers. Second, the American public became significantly more affluent. Third, alcohol products relative to all other consumer goods became substantially less expensive. Finally, advertising exploded both in terms of the number of channels available to reach and persuade consumers and the amount of resources manufacturers were willing to commit to advertising. Thus, we see an increase in the heaviest consuming segment of the population, consumers who can more easily afford alcohol products just as they are becoming cheaper when compared with other consumer products, and industry having greater ability and willingness to communicate with consumers. In effect then, we see a number of reinforcing trends, which individually and in concert should have promoted increased consumption of alcoholic beverages and total alcohol.

Yet, while the effect of these trends on consumption should be unidirectional,

Figure 2.6
Share of Deflated Total Media Spending

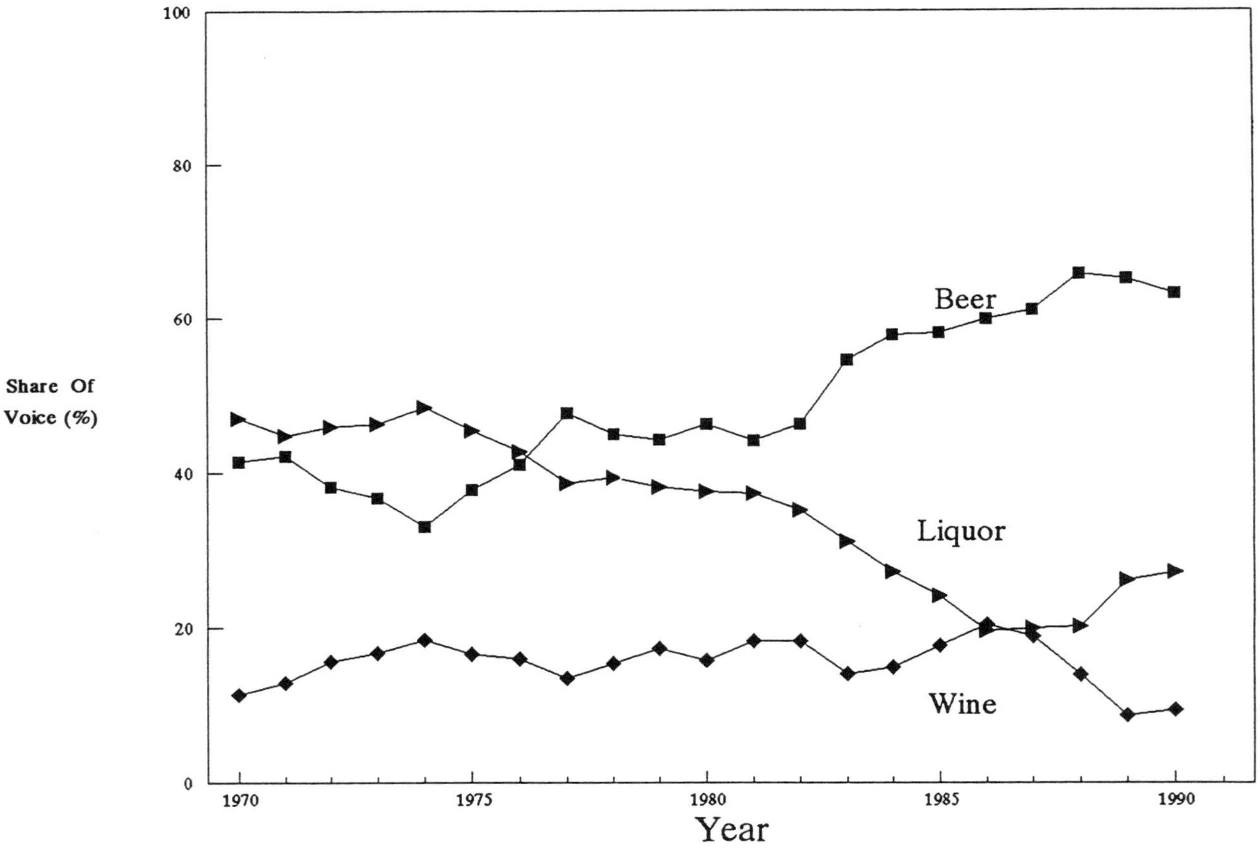

they appear to work at cross-purposes when we consider category consumption. For instance, the growth of the 20- to 34-year-old segment of the population should favor beer consumption and to a lesser degree wine drinking versus consumption of liquor products. Similarly, the growth of advertising spending and especially beer share of voice should help increase beer drinking again shifting share away from liquor products. Economic factors create counteracting pressure, however. In this instance, growing consumer affluence should put more expensive liquor products within reach of more consumers. Further the relative decline in prices was greatest for liquor products. Increasing wealth and declining prices should have helped shift share of consumption to liquor products from the other alcoholic beverage options, as a result. We will see next which of these trends wins out.

The descriptive statistics for consumption by beverage category and in total as well as share of total consumption by source are given in Table 2.3. From the table it can be seen that on average over the four decades studied, every person in the United States above the age of 14 consumed 2.4 gallons of absolute alcohol every year. This translates into approximately 307 ounces of raw alcohol or just under one ounce per day per adult. Of this total about half, 48.9% was sourced from beer consumption. Beer drinking contributed 1.18 gallons of absolute alcohol per adult per year, 151 ounces or an ounce per person every other day. Immediately behind beer was liquor consumption which represented 39.4% of all alcohol ingested. On a volumetric basis, liquor drinking was the source of nearly a gallon, .948, of absolute alcohol consumption per adult per year. Finally, alcohol ingestion from wine drinking represented just 11.7% of all the alcohol consumed or .286 gallons per adult per year.

If we examine the trend over time (Figure 2.7), we can see that total adult per capita consumption hovered at about two gallons a year for the decades of the 1950s. Total consumption rose slowly and steadily for the next 20 years reaching a peak of almost three gallons per adult per year, 2.82 gallons on average. Total consumption then declined throughout the decade of the 1980s ending at about 2.5 gallons per adult per year or roughly the mean level for the entire 40-year period. It is also interesting to note that the 40% growth in consumption appears to closely parallel the increase in the young adult segment of the population (Figure 2.2) and the decline in relative prices of alcohol products (Figure 2.4) but is less closely akin to increases in affluence (Figure 2.3) or advertising (Figure 2.5).

On a category level, the biggest changes over time affect beer and liquor consumption. With respect to the former, consumption of alcohol from beer drinking held at roughly one gallon per adult per year from 1950–1965. Thereafter it increased by roughly 50% growing to 1.4 gallons by 1980 and staying at that level for the next ten years. Liquor consumption, by comparison, rose from 1950 until 1975, growing from .73 gallons per year per adult to 1.15 gallons. From 1975 onward, there was a significant decline in alcohol consumption from drinking liquor products and this reduction accounted for nearly

Table 2.3
Descriptive Statistics for Consumption

Annual Alcohol Consumption (Gallons of Alcohol Per Capita 15)	Mean	Standard Deviation	Low	High	Years
Beer	1.180	.165	.96	1.42	41
Wine	.286	.063	.20	.40	41
Liquor	.948	.141	.73	1.15	41
Total	2.413	.312	1.96	2.82	41
Share of Consumption (%)					
Beer	48.9	2.80	44.5	54.7	41
Wine	11.7	1.44	9.9	15.1	41
Liquor	39.4	3.79	31.8	45.0	41

Figure 2.7
Per Capita Alcohol Consumption

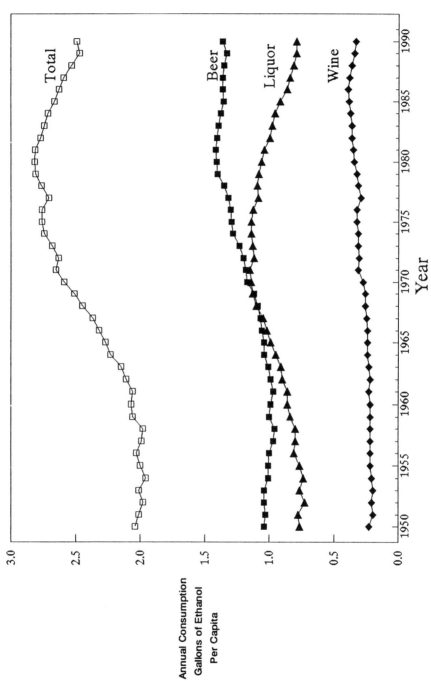

all the decline in total alcohol consumption over the same period. Lastly, wine consumption seems to change very little over time but the trend in Figure 2.7 belies what in fact is a doubling of alcohol consumption from wine drinking. In 1950, absolute alcohol consumption from wine drinking was .20 gallons a year and it peaked at .40 gallons per year in 1986.

Category shares of total consumption are also given in Table 2.3 and are graphically depicted in Figure 2.8. On average, nearly half of all alcohol consumption, 48.9%, was sourced from beer drinking. Liquor drinking contributed the next largest share of total consumption, 39.4%, while wine drinking share of total consumption was 11.7%. However, these average figures hide the major share dynamic present in the data. Over time there has been a nearly equivalent trade-off in liquor share for beer share. Thus, beer share began the period well above liquor share, 51.0% versus 37.7%. Beer share declined subsequently while liquor share increased until parity was reached in 1970. Beer share rose steadily over the next 20 years as liquor share fell. By 1990 beer share stood at 54.7% and liquor share at 31.8%. A portion of the lost liquor share was absorbed by wine consumption, which increased by 52.5% growing from 9.9% share to 15.1%.

It is interesting again to visually compare the trends in Figure 2.8 with those for the predictor variables. It would seem that demographic trends are associated with the growth in beer and wine share at the expense of liquor. On the surface, this relationship would tend to confirm the belief of marketers that beer and wine are the preferred drinks of young consumers and liquor tends to be favored by more mature segments. Growth in personal disposable income and declines in relative prices do not seem to be related in any obvious manner to the changes in share. Advertising and in particular share of voice (Figure 2.6) seems to follow the same pattern most noticeably for beer and liquor. It remains then for the statistical analyses reported in Chapters 3 and 4 to sort out which of these apparent relationships is statistically significant and to quantify the strength of the relationship.

SUMMARY

In this chapter we have described the data that will be used to estimate demand models for consumption and share of consumption. The source of each data element was documented as were any limitations with the way a particular variable was measured, most noticeably the various specifications that were possible for advertising. Additionally, the data were described in a descriptive sense to provide a context for the more sophisticated analyses that will be presented in later chapters.

In total five general types of data will be included in the demand model: a demographic indicator—the number of 20- to 34-year-olds in the population; a measure of consumer affluence—deflated personal disposable income expressed on a per capita adult basis where adult is defined to be 15 years or older; relative

Figure 2.8
Share of Alcohol Consumption

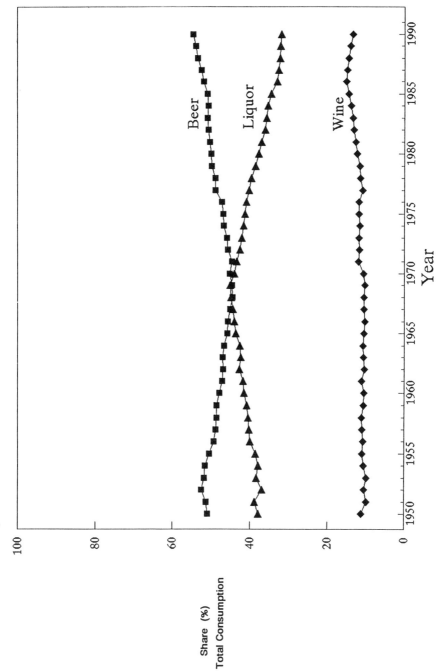

Share (%)
Total Consumption

Beer

Liquor

Wine

Year

price—the indexed price of an alcoholic beverage category, for example, beer, expressed as a ratio of the Consumer Price Index for all consumer goods; advertising—deflated spending for the three beverage categories in magazines and magazine pages for the entire study period and deflated spending in six media and in total from 1970 through 1990; and lastly, a linear trend defined by the year for which data were measured. For the outcome measures, consumption figures were available for each of the three beverage types and in total. These figures were used, in turn, to calculate shares of total consumption for the three alcoholic beverage types. All consumption figures were expressed as gallons of raw or absolute alcohol consumed per adult (15 years or over) per year.

When we examined these variables individually a number of interesting and potentially important trends were apparent. First, there was a dramatic increase in the young adult population of the country. The 20- to 34-year-old segment doubled over time from 33.6 million to 63.1 million as the post–World War II baby boom came of age and became legal drinkers. As young adults are typically the heaviest per capita consumers of alcoholic beverages we might expect total consumption to rise as a consequence. Further, young drinkers demonstrate a decided preference for malt beverages and to a lesser degree wine over distilled spirits alternatives. We might expect to see significant share changes coincident with the demographic trend therefore.

Over the four decades studied, the American public became substantially more affluent. Per capita personal disposable income doubled in real terms from just under $8,000 per year to almost $16,000. There is considerable evidence in the econometric literature on demand for alcohol products that consumers spent a fairly constant portion of their discretionary income on alcohol products. If this were true over time in the United States, the personal disposable income figures would suggest that American adults could spend twice as much on alcoholic beverages while maintaining an historical share of household budgets reserved for these purchases. Again, we might expect that increased consumption could be the result. As for share of consumption, increases in discretionary income would tend to favor products that are traditionally the most expensive, liquor and wine, as they come within reach of a larger proportion of the population.

At the same time that Americans could better afford alcoholic beverages, the prices of the products were falling relative to other consumer products. At the start of the period the index for liquor products was twice the CPI while beer and wine indices were 50% above the index for other consumer goods. By 1990 relative liquor prices had fallen 60% and beer and wine prices 40% such that the indexed price of the three beverages was less than the CPI for other consumer products. Declining relative prices would make alcohol products more attractive when compared with other nonalcoholic alternatives and we could forecast a consequent pressure toward greater consumption. As for share of consumption, liquor prices declined the most and ended the study period comparably priced with alcoholic beverage substitutes. In effect, the relative price differential was removed although liquor prices undoubtedly remained higher than beer or wine in absolute terms. Nonetheless, price changes should have served to stimulate liquor consumption more than beer or wine drinking.

Advertising is the last predictor variable considered and here again we see dramatic changes over time. Specifically, media usage by manufacturers is typified by two major trends: a tremendous growth in real advertising spending for alcoholic beverage products, especially beer, and the development of new media channels to reach consumers. A good indication of the first point is what has happened to spending in all media since 1970. Real advertising spending for beer products tripled rising from $181.4 million to $639.4 million. Over the same period wine also tripled from a low spending level of $67.8 million to a high of $215.2 million and liquor advertising spending varied from $197.2 million to $371.1 million. As for advertising for all alcoholic beverages, 1970 spending was $446.4 million and by the late 1980s it too had tripled to nearly one and a quarter billion dollars, $1,226 million.

Combined with the real growth in advertising was a proliferation of media options in which messages could be conveyed. It is significant that advertising in only one medium, magazines, could be tracked for the entire duration of study. By 1990 ten media were routinely monitored and of these four were measured for six or fewer years. Thus, manufacturers were presented with more ways to reach consumers just as their willingness to spend corporate resources to persuade consumers was also increasing.

Unlike some of the other predictors, however, the impact of advertising on alcohol consumption is not immediately obvious. If advertising was spent primarily on individual product appeals, the impact might be expected within category only and hence there would be limited impact on total consumption. Similarly, a preponderance of spending for products in one category versus another, say beer as compared with liquor, might shift category shares while leaving total consumption unchanged. On the other hand, advertising might reinforce drinking or stimulate greater consumption for every drinking occasion. Thus, we might argue convincingly that advertising had no effect on total alcohol consumption or conversely that it did indeed promote increased consumption.

The effect of advertising on category shares is less difficult to predict, however. Looking at share of total advertising, or as it is known among media professionals share of voice by beverage category (Figure 2.6) it would appear that beer share of voice increased over the last 15 years of the study period at the expense of liquor share. If advertising is influential in determining category shares then we might expect the share of total alcohol consumption sourced from beer drinking to grow over time and this growth would be offset by declines in the proportionate amount of total alcohol consumption coming from liquor drinking.

In concert the four primary determinants of alcohol demand would seem to create a substantial push toward greater alcohol consumption by the average adult American. The heaviest drinking segment of the population was growing in size and influence at the same time that alcohol products were becoming more affordable due to the greater affluence of the public and the decline in relative prices of alcoholic beverage products. Manufacturers' ability and willingness to reach and persuade consumers grew apace. The pressure to consume more alcohol per capita seems almost irresistible, therefore, as a function of the broad social and economic trends.

And indeed, total alcohol consumption did increase over the four decades studied. Total absolute alcohol consumption averaged 2.4 gallons per adult per year but more importantly grew by 43.9% from a low of 1.96 gallons annually per capita to a high of 2.82 gallons. Beer appeared to benefit most in volumetric terms from the upward trend increasing from a low of .96 gallons of raw alcohol per year to a high of 1.42 gallons. Wine grew the most on a percentage basis, doubling from .2 gallons to .4 gallons per year. Alcohol consumption from liquor drinking increased modestly from 1950 to 1970 and subsequently declined approximately its starting level of .73 gallons.

Share of total consumption by beverage type was equally revealing. Liquor consumption declined inexorably over the last two decades of the study period, from a 45 share to just under 32. This decline was paralleled by a near equal gain in beer consumption which grew 10 share points from 44.5% to 54.7%. To a lesser degree, wine consumption replaced liquor drinking; wine share grew from 9.9% to 15.1% over the study period.

When we visually compare the trends in social and economic factors with the pattern of consumption it would appear that demographic shifts most closely fit the changes in consumption totally and on a category basis, since younger consumers drink more and prefer beer and wine to liquor. Economic factors and advertising also appear to promote increased alcohol consumption, but tend to negate the demographic affects on a category level. Whereas the growth of the young adult segment would seem to favor beer and wine consumption, the greater affluence of the public and drop in relative prices, especially for distilled spirits would seem to promote liquor consumption more than wine and beer. Advertising, specifically share of voice, also appears to positively impact beer share at the expense of liquor. We will investigate the effect of these gross trends on alcohol consumption and endeavor to sort out the competing effects on a category level in the next two chapters.

Chapter 3

Alcohol Consumption

In this chapter we will consider how consumption of alcohol, by beverage type and total, has varied in the United States since 1950. Second, the factors that are related to alcohol consumption over time will be identified and the strength of the relationship will be quantified. Of particular interest will be whether or not advertising for alcoholic beverage products is related to consumption of an individual alcohol product type such as beer or wine or if it is associated with a significant increase in total alcohol consumption when other factors that affect demand are controlled.

The first section of the chapter summarizes the demand models for consumption, and the second examines share of consumption. In these analyses we investigate each beverage type individually and attempt to determine how it is related to factors that influence demand for alcohol products. The third section of the chapter considers total alcohol consumption as a system; that is, how the demand predictors are related to individual alcohol beverage consumption and total consumption simultaneously.

It is important when reviewing the results to recall the statistical analyses, no matter how seemingly sophisticated, are ultimately correlational in nature. Hence, we are measuring how closely the movement of one series, say beer consumption, parallels that of another such as price. We may impute a logical causality but no temporal one is assumed. To look for time-ordered effects the series have been examined for time series structure, in particular crosscorrelation leads and lags. Further, we noted in the preceding chapter some of the problems inherent in using magazine spending as the measure of advertising. To minimize this source of bias the demand models have been rerun with three other measurements of advertising, Magazine Pages, Total 6 Media, and Total Media. The time series and corroborative media analyses are presented in the last section of the chapter.

CONSUMPTION

Table 3.1 presents the results of the primary demand models for each of the three beverage classes. Each demand model consists of a trend factor, Year, a demographic indictor of heavy users, Population, and a measure of personal disposable income, Income. Additionally, the relative price index, Price, and the advertising measure, Magazine Ad $, specific to each beverage type is included in its demand model only.

Another important feature of the analysis is that the regressions have been centered. That is, the intercept term, b_0, is the grand mean of the dependent variable. As an example, the intercept for beer consumption given in Table 3.1 is 1.191 suggesting over the 38 years studied the average annual adult per capita ingestion of ethanol is 1.191 gallons from beer drinking. The comparable figures for wine and liquor are .321 and .963 gallons, respectively.[1]

Centering makes the regression coefficients produced by the demand models immediately interpretable. Each coefficient measures the change in average annual adult alcohol consumption for a particular beverage that results from a unit change in the predictor variable, holding all other predictors constant at their mean. Returning again to Table 3.1, note that the regression coefficient for Year in the beer consumption model is -.020. This estimate indicates that over the time period studied, annual beer consumption by adults declined, resulting in an average yearly decrease of .020 gallons of alcohol consumed from this source, holding the effects of other demand predictors constant. Similarly, a coefficient of .009 for Population suggests that for every additional 1 million people in the population who are 20 to 34 years old the average per capita consumption of alcohol, derived from beer drinking, will increase .009 gallons per year. With these interpretative guidelines in mind, we can now consider the demand models.

Beer consumption by adults from 1953 to 1990 is significantly related to Population, Income, Price, and Year. Just as importantly, it is not related to the amount of advertising spending in magazines over the same period. As noted above, the relationship for Year is negative, indicating falling per capita beer consumption over time, whereas it is positive for Population, suggesting that beer consumption increases on average with the size of the 20- to 34-year-old segment of the population.

As would be predicted by economic theory, Income is positively related to beer consumption and the relationship with Price is negative. Interpreting the regression coefficient for Income, average annual per capita alcohol consumption increases .004 gallons for every ten constant dollars of disposable income adults gain.[2] The average personal disposable income for the time period studied was $12,116.60 in 1982 dollars and if that figure grew by 10% or $1,212, beer

Table 3.I
Regression Models for Consumption

		Beer b	Beer t	Wine b	Wine t	Liquor b	Liquor t
	Year	-.020	-3.86*	-.004	-.50	-.040	-4.01*
	Population	.009	2.67*	.007	2.49*	-.036	-2.10*
	Income	.004	2.90*	.001	.49	.014	4.77*
Price Index	Beer	-1.037	-3.78*				
	Wine			.018	.13		
	Liquor					-1.175	-2.48*
Magazine Ad $	Beer	-.020	-.24				
	Wine			-.112	-.68		
	Liquor					.150	4.00*
	b_0	1.191	250.30*	.321	93.83*	.963	84.83*
	R^2	.973		.893		.768	
	Adj R^2	.969		.867		.732	

*$p < .05$

consumption would increase absolute alcohol ingestion per adult by .485 gallons per year (.004 x 121.2) all other influences held constant.

By comparison, the coefficient for Price is -1.037. Since Price is a relative measure its interpretation is less direct and requires some care. So, a unit change in the predictor variable suggests the relative price of a product increases or decreases 100% of the CPI. The coefficient implies that should the price index of beer rise by 10% relative to the movement in Consumer Price Index, beer consumption would decline by an amount equal to .104 gallons of alcohol per adult per year (.10* -1.037). Conversely, a decline in relative price, which in fact describes the historical experience of beer prices, would increase beer consumption, again a 10% decline in relative price equating to an increase of .104 gallons of ethanol per adult per year.

The demand model provides a good fit to the data, accounting for 97.3% of the variability in beer consumption, 96.9% on an adjusted basis. Even so, high R^2s are typical of regressions using short time series when the values of most variables are moving monotonically and hence the strength of the relationship should be viewed with some caution.

More problematical is the extent of multicollinearity among the predictor variables. The standardized regression coefficients, betas, are large and even exceed 1 in two cases making them effectively meaningless. The standardized coefficients are clearly distorted by multicollinearity and should not be interpreted; they have been omitted from Table 3.1 as a consequence. Nevertheless, the unstandardized or raw regression coefficients, bs, remain accurate and unbiased estimates of the relationship between a demand predictor and consumption, albeit not precise ones, and are included in the table as are the tests of significance, which tend to be conservative when data are ill-conditioned with multicollinearity.[3] Other steps have been taken to remove multicollinearity by factor analyzing regressor variables and by taking first differences. These analyses will be described later.

Returning to Table 3.1 the demand model for wine was constrained to a 27-year period by the lack of price data. Over this period, the average annual adult ingestion of alcohol from wine consumption was .321 gallons. From the regression model, specifically the coefficient for Year, it can be seen then per capita consumption declined slowly over the time period studied. The average annual decrease in consumption, -.004 gallons, was not statistically significant however.

Among the predictor variables only Population is significantly related to wine consumption. According to the regression coefficient alcohol, consumption sourced from wine increases by .007 gallons per adult per year with each additional 1 million 20- to 34-year-olds in the population. The signs of the supply and demand variables, Income and Price, are as predicted by economic theory, positive and negative, respectively, but neither comes remotely close to being statistically significant. Advertising is also not significant and the sign of the regression coefficient is counterintuitive.

The liquor consumption time series was available for 38 years. Over the study period, annual adult alcohol consumption from liquor averaged .963 gallons. Consumption additionally declined rapidly and significantly, .040 gallons per person per year all other factors held constant. Controlling other influences, alcohol consumption from liquor would have declined from approximately 1.72 gallons at the beginning of the period to .20 gallons at the end.

Liquor consumption appears to be strongly affected by other demand predictors as well. For example, the coefficient for Population in Table 3.1 is -.036, indicating that liquor consumption declines as the number of 20- to 34-year-olds in the population increases. This finding confirms the marketing maxim that liquor preference and consumption is greatest among older segments of the population. Additionally, the corresponding coefficients for Population in the beer and wine models reveals that some of the decline in liquor consumption associated with more 20- to 34-year-olds in the country is offset by gains in beer and wine consumption, .016 gallons to be precise. The three regression coefficients vividly illustrate the need to study all alcoholic beverages as a system and the erroneous conclusions that might result if they are not.

The classic economic demand predictors are strongly related to liquor consumption. Alcohol ingestion from liquor drinking rises with disposable income, .014 gallons per adult per year with each $10 additional in per capita-deflated income, and falls with relative price. The regression coefficient for Price also suggests that if the price of liquor increased by 10% relative to the CPI, alcohol consumption would decline .117 gallons per person per year. Conversely, a decrease in relative price by 50%, an historical fact, should have increased liquor consumption by an average of .587 gallons of ethanol per adult per year, other effects held constant.

For the first time, advertising matters in the liquor demand model. In particular, the regression coefficient for Magazine Ad $ suggests that for each additional 1 million constant dollars in liquor advertising, raw alcohol consumption will increase .150 gallons per adult annually on average. This finding is subject, of course, to the usual provisos, namely advertising dollars are deflated and other demand influences are held constant.

To summarize the findings to this point, the demand models for the three alcoholic beverage categories are quite consistent in many respects. Regardless of type of beverage alcohol consumption per adult has declined, .04 gallons per adult per year from liquor drinking and .02 and .004 gallons per adult per year from beer and wine drinking, respectively. Increases in the heavy drinking segment of the population affect all three demand models, with beer and wine consumption growing as the number of 20- to 34-year-olds in the population rises. Consumption of raw alcohol from these two sources is partially offset by the decline in liquor drinking that is associated with a growth in the heavy user segment. The classic demand predictors of economic theory, price and income, work as expected—as a depressant and stimulant to consumption respectively—and are significantly related to alcohol consumption sourced from beer and liquor drinking. Finally, advertising appears to be only related to liquor consumption with greater advertising spending in real terms being related to increases in liquor consumption. What remains unclear is if the lack of an advertising relationship with beer and wine consumption is indeed an accurate reflection of reality or is instead due to the fact that so little beer and wine advertising spending is in magazines.

SHARE OF CONSUMPTION

Table 3.2 summarized the regression model for the three beverage categories when demand is expressed as a share of total consumption. This specification adds unique and valuable information that is not available when the models examine consumption by beverage type in volumetric terms. Most importantly, total consumption is treated as a constant summing to 100% in every year. The variability in the time series is then the mix of beverage shares that make up total consumption.

The principal consequences of treating demand as a share of total consumption are twofold. First, share of consumption measures shifts in consumer preference for various beverage types over time. Shares view consumption as a closed system of consumer choices and hence a gain by one beverage category is accompanied by a commensurate decline in some combination of the other consumption options. It is possible then to determine how variability in consumption of one class of beverage affects consumption of the others.

Further, the regression coefficients produced by the demand models represent the effect of a predictor on the system of shares. That is, although each share of consumption model is estimated separately for each beverage option, the coefficient for every predictor measures a trade-off in preference of one beverage type in relation to another. The coefficient for any predictor is not fully understandable in the context of a single demand model but instead its full influence on consumption can only be seen by comparing coefficients across the three share of consumption demand models. For this reason, the three models given in Table 3.2 are interpreted together in the discussion that follows.

As before, the demand models have been centered such that the intercept is the mean share of consumption of each beverage over the time series. Note then in Table 3.2 beer consumption represented roughly 48.7% of all alcohol consumption on average during the term of study. The corresponding average shares for wine and liquor consumption were 12.3% and 39.5%, respectively. Under normal circumstances the intercepts, b_0, should sum to 100 instead of 100.5. However, because of the lack of price data, the wine series is shorter than those of beer and liquor and the intercepts do not add exactly to 100.

The regression coefficients, in turn, measure change in share of consumption for a particular beverage that occurs with a unit change in a predictor variable when other factors are held constant at their mean level. As noted earlier, the coefficients also measure the trade-off in consumer preference that occurs with

Table 3.2
Regression Models for Share of Consumption

		Beer		Wine		Liquor	
		b	t	b	t	b	t
Year		.495	1.62	-.042	-.15	-.552	-2.90*
Population		.570	3.02*	.047	.46	-1.059	-3.25*
Income		-.207	-2.68*	.019	.37	.224	3.97*
Price Index	Beer	33.201	2.08*				
	Wine			-6.205	-1.19		
	Liquor					-21.419	-2.40*
Magazine Ad $	Beer	-1.150	-.24				
	Wine			-6.010	-.95		
	Liquor					3.078	4.36*
b_0		48.689	176.28*	12.261	94.53*	39.487	183.35*
R^2		.678		.838		.900	
Adj R^2		.628		.800		.885	

*$p < .05$

changes in a predictor variable. A single contributor to demand such as Income can be expected to have contradictory effects on different beverage categories as the impact on one type of beverage trades off against consumption of the others. This can lead to seemingly counterintuitive findings in some cases.

The coefficients for Year in the three models provide a good illustration of the interplay between beverage categories and the need to explain effects jointly. The coefficient for beer share indicates that, all other factors held constant, beer consumption increases .495 share points per year on average. Hence, beer is gaining as the alcoholic beverage of choice over time. Wine by comparison is largely unchanged falling a mere .042 share points per year on average. The share of total consumption represented by wine drinking varies in a narrow range, ± .55 share points around the mean level of 12.26%. Beer consumption gained share as a consequence almost exclusively at the expense of liquor consumption which dropped .552 share points per year on average.

With respect to Population, beer share increases with the number of 20- to 34-year-olds in the population. Specifically, the beer share of total consumption increases .57 points for every million 20- to 34-year-olds in the country. The effect of Population on wine consumption is negligible, .047 points, and again gain in beer share comes mostly at the expense of decreases in liquor consumption. Liquor share declines by just over a share point, 1.059, for each additional million 20- to 34-year-olds in the country. These findings confirm the belief that beer is the alcoholic beverage of choice for younger consumers while preference for liquor grows as a share of total consumption with age.

Considering Income, liquor consumption appears to be the most sensitive to changes in consumer affluence. Liquor share of total consumption increases .224 points for every $10 of additional personal disposable income adults in the United States have. Beer consumption evidences a reciprocal decline, -.207 points, with rising wealth. Thus, the more affluent consumers become, the more likely they will buy distilled spirits as the alcoholic beverage of choice moving away from malt beverages primarily.

The coefficient for Price and Magazine Ad $ differ from the previous estimates in that they were not measured uniformly for each beverage type. The trade-offs between categories are less direct therefore even though systemwide effects are still in evidence. For instance, liquor and wine shares operate with respect to Price as might be expected from demand theory. That is, both shares decline as the price of the beverage increases relative to the CPI. According to the regression coefficients, liquor share could be expected to drop 21.42 points or 54.2% of its average level if its relative price were to double. Similarly, if the relative price of wine doubled, its share would drop 6.01 points or 49.0% of its average.

Beer share, by contrast, varies directly with price, the coefficient suggesting that a doubling in relative price would actually be associated with a gain in share. This finding is clearly an artifact of expressing the dependent variable as a percentage of total consumption. Liquor consumption is more price sensitive than is beer consumption. Over time, the relative price of all alcoholic beverages has dropped but especially liquor price, which fell by more than half over the period. Beer price also dropped but to a lesser degree. The increase in liquor and wine share with lower prices had to be reflected somewhere and appeared therefore as an opposite movement in beer shares. Consequently, when liquor and wine share grow as price declines, a spurious effect is seen in beer shares, which appear to grow with higher relative price when in reality beer share is simply less sensitive to price shifts.

The cross-category effects of Magazine Ad $ are even more ambiguous. For all three categories of alcoholic beverages relative price fell over time. Since all prices were moving in the same general direction there were still substitution effects across beverage categories, albeit not nearly perfect ones as were evinced for Year, Population, and Income. Magazine advertising is more variable and does not correspond exactly across categories and the trade-off between beverage share is not direct.

Advertising influences only liquor share significantly. The regression coefficient measuring the relationship between Magazine Ad $ and liquor share suggests that an additional advertising expenditure of one million in 1982 constant dollars would increase liquor share by 3.078 points. The coefficients for Magazine Ad $ in the wine share and beer share models have negative signs, suggesting that share decreases with increases in advertising. But then, neither of these relationships is remotely close to being statistically significant.

To summarize the major findings coming from the share of consumption regressions, it appears initially that the primary trade-off is between beer and liquor, the size and signs of the coefficients being nearly mirror images of each other. Beer share, as an example, grows at an annual rate of .495 points and liquor share declines an almost equal amount, on average .552 points. Wine share remains very stable over time and is largely unaffected by demand influences. Both beer and liquor share are sensitive to shifts in the age composition of the country, beer consumption increasing as the number of 20- to 34-year-olds grows and liquor share declining. Liquor share appears to be more sensitive to classic demand predictors, increasing with the wealth of consumers and declining with the relative price of products. Movement in beer share as it is related to Income and Price seem to be largely accounted for by opposition to liquor share changes. With respect to advertising, liquor share is positively and significantly affected by increases in magazine advertising expenditures whereas beer and wine shares of total consumption are unaffected by advertising spending in magazines.

FACTOR ANALYTIC REGRESSIONS

The correlation matrix used in the demand regressions and the standardized regression coefficients, betas, indicate the presence of a high degree of multicollinearity among the predictor variables. As with many time series analyses, the predictor variables are moving in the same direction over the period studied at roughly proportional rates. Consequently, many of the predictors provide little unique information, and their independent contribution to demand is difficult to assess.

One method to deal with multicollinearity in a data set is to combine the collinear variables along a single dimension by means of factor analysis. The resulting composite variable is representative of an underlying construct or dimension that the predictor variables individually measure to an imperfect degree. Yearly values for the composite variable can be used as predictors in the demand model replacing the collinear variables. The factor analytic solution has the added benefit that the values for the composite variable, the factor scores, are orthogonal, that is, they are uncorrelated and hence the unique and completely independent contribution of the composite variable on demand can be assessed.

On the outcome side, we have been concerned with how demand for the three beverage types operate as a system of consumer preferences. Systemwide effects were approximated by expressing beverage class consumption as a share of total consumption. This transformation enables us to examine the consumption trade-offs between beverage types and what factors affect the movement from one type of alcoholic beverage to another. The analysis is always constrained to a constant, 100%, however, and it is not possible using shares to comprehend changes in total alcohol consumption. Ultimately, it is increases or decreases in average raw alcohol consumption that will be manifest in morbidity and morality rates if the single distribution theory is accurate.

Again, factor analysis provides an alternative that enables us to examine both systemwide effects and changes in absolute alcohol consumption. In this case, the four consumption statistics—annual adult per capita beer, wine, liquor, and total consumption figures—are factor analyzed. The resulting factor dimensions indicate which consumption figures are moving together and hence which beverage types are compliments, which are moving in opposition and are substitutes, and most importantly how the changes in each beverage type is related to total consumption.

The final stage of the analysis is to relate the two sets of factor scores in a regression model. Scores from each of the factors of the outcome variables, the underlying dimensions of consumption, are regressed in turn on the factor scores of the composite variables that describe the structural dimensions of the demand predictors. In the end, systemwide variability among alcohol beverage types and total consumption are related to the demand predictors through the intermediate stage of the newly constructed factor variable.

To summarize then, three factor analyses have been performed: (1) of the demand predictors, (2) all four consumption measures, and (3) the three share measures combined with total consumption. Two regression analyses were then conducted, first of the consumption factors on the demand predictor factors and subsequently of the share of consumption and total consumption factors or the demand predictor factors. In the discussion, results of the three factor analyses are given initially followed by the factor analytic regressions for consumption and the share of consumption.

Table 3.3 summarizes the results of the factor analysis of the demand predictors. Note that wine price has been deleted from the analysis. This was done to maximize the length of time studied since the inclusion of wine price would have limited the time series to 27 rather than 38 years. Additionally, the simple bivariate correlation between beer price and wine price is .91, indicating that 83% of the variability in wine price is described by beer price fluctuations. Little is lost by using beer price as a proxy for wine price then, and much is gained in the length of the time series that can be analyzed.

The second important feature of the factor analysis is that two indicators of advertising can be included, Magazine Ad $ and Magazine Pages. Previously, deflated magazine spending was used as the indicator of beverage category advertising. Because the factor analysis will collapse variables that are highly correlated into a single dimension, there is no loss of efficiency in using several means of measuring the same construct. Quite the contrary, the factor solution is improved by adding a number of ways to characterize the same phenomenon since the underlying dimension is measured more accurately.

Returning to the results given in Table 3.3, we can see that the factor solution isolates three structural dimensions in the predictor data set. The first of these accounting for 60.3% of the variability in the predictors is labeled Trend and measures the monotonic movement in a number of predictors over time. As can be seen from the correlations of the original variables with the dimension, the factor loadings, Population, .98, and Income, .87, are increasing in a nearly linear fashion over the study period while prices of beer, -.96, and liquor, -.97, are declining linearly. Year measures the simple linear trend in the data and the factor loading of .95 suggests that it also describes the first factor quite well. In fact, 90% of the variability in the structural dimension is attributable to the linear trend in the data.

The second factor measures advertising for liquor and wine. Of the two beverage types, wine is more closely associated with the factor since the factor loadings, i.e., the correlations of the raw data with the factor, for both Magazine Ad $ and Magazine Pages is .90. The factor loadings for liquor advertising are considerably lower, .82 for Magazine Ad $ and .58 for Magazine Pages. Much of the remaining variability in liquor advertising is explained by the first factor, Trend, and in fact, Magazine Pages is more closely associated with the first factor than the second by virtue of the .64 loading. So 41% of the variability in liquor advertising as measured by the number of magazine pages is due to a simple increase year over year. Overall, the second factor explains 15.7% of the variability in the predictor variables.

The last factor, representing 15.1% of the variability in the original data, is associated with beer advertising. Both Magazine Ad $ and Magazine Pages load highly on the last factor, .92 and .90, respectively. The three factors when summed account for 91% of the variability in the predictor variables.

Table 3.3
Factor Analysis of Demand Predictors

		Trend	Wine & Liquor Advertising	Beer Advertising
	Year	.95	.26	.05
	Population	.98	.18	.02
	Income	.87	.34	−.03
Price Index	Beer	−.96	−.25	.00
	Liquor	−.97	−.22	−.01
	Beer	−.31	.08	.92
Magazine Ad $	Wine	.24	.90	.14
	Liquor	.41	.82	−.02
	Beer	.31	−.08	.90
Magazine Pages	Wine	.14	.90	−.08
	Liquor	.64	.58	−.13
Variance (%)		60.3	15.6	15.1
Cum Variance (%)		60.3	75.9	91.0

The second factor analysis of annual consumption statistics is given in Table 3.4. In this instance two factors describe the data almost completely. The first of these, accounting for just over three quarters (77.8%) of all the variability in consumption is associated with beer and wine consumption, which have correlations with the factor of .97 and .98, respectively. About 95% of the variability in both wine and beer consumption is accounted for by the factor dimension. Because both beverages are positively associated with the factor, the two alcoholic beverage forms are moving in the same manner over time, suggesting that beer and wine may be compliments or at least are affected in a like manner by demand influences.

The second factor describes liquor consumption nearly perfectly. The factor loading of .99 shows that 98% of the variability in liquor consumption is described by the derived factor. Because liquor loads almost exclusively on a factor that is independent of both beer and wine consumption, it suggests that while liquor is not precisely a substitute for the other beverages (if it were liquor consumption would load on the first factor with a negative sign) it definitely moves differently over time. It may as a result be affected by different demand predictors or have differential sensitivity to them when compared with beer and wine consumption.

The most interesting aspect of the factor solution involves total consumption. Just under two-thirds of the variability in total consumption (65.6%) is associated with changes in beer and wine consumption as shown by the loading of .81 on the first factor. Virtually all of the remaining variance, 33.6%, is associated with liquor consumption by virtue of the total consumption loading of .58 on the second factor.

With respect to the total variability in the consumption variables, 20.8% is explained by the second factor and as noted above 77.8% was described by the first. Combined the two factors account for 98.6% of the variance in all consumption measures during the study period. In short, the factor analytic solution preserves almost all the information in the original consumption data set.

The third and final factor analysis is shown in Table 3.5 and includes the three measures of beverage share with total consumption. The data set is completely described by a three-factor solution. The first of these, accounting for nearly seven-tenths (69.5%) of the variability in all the variables, is attributable to a trade-off in share between beer and liquor consumption. In particular, beer share has a factor loading of .98 and liquor -.90. This factor indicates that nearly all of the variability in beer share (96%) can be accounted for by reciprocal movements in liquor, beer share gaining when liquor falls and vice versa. Note also that wine share has a loading of .54 on the first factor indicating that 29.2% of its variability is also associated with movements in opposition to liquor. The factor loading of -.90 suggests that 81% of the variability in liquor share is accounted for with movement in opposition to beer primarily and wine secondarily. These findings suggest that liquor is to some degree a substitute for beer and wine which may, in turn, be at least partial compliments.

Table 3.4
Factor Analysis of Consumption

	Beer, Wine & Total	Liquor & Total
Beer	.97	. 20
Wine	.98	. 13
Liquor	. 17	.99
Total	.81	. 58
Variance (%)	77.8	20.9
Cum Variance (%)	77.8	98.7

Perhaps the most fascinating finding related to the first factor is that total consumption has a near trivial loading of .03 and just .09% of the variability is accounted for by the factor. In essence then all the movement in shares between beverage types accounting for 96% of the variability in beer share, 81% in liquor and 29% in wine, has no bearing on total consumption. This result demonstrates quite dramatically that movement to and from beverage categories has limited impact on total alcohol consumption. These findings are consistent then with the belief that advertising effects, should they be seen to influence one beverage category, dissipate systemwide, thereby attenuating their impact on total consumption.

As for total consumption, it loads almost exclusively on the second factor, .98, which would therefore account for 96% of its variability. Beer and liquor shares are virtually unrelated to this factor, .04% and 2.0% of the variability, respectively. Wine share interestingly is more closely related to total consumption with 16% of its variability accounted for by the factor. Nevertheless, the second factor again illustrates that the category share wars have almost no impact on total consumption.

The last factor is associated with wine share movements, suggesting that wine to some degree follows an independent course relative to the other beverage types. In fact, the factor loading of .74 indicates that 54.8% of the variability in wine share is due to the factor. Of the other beverage types only liquor share has a meaningful loading of -.41 or 16.8% of its variability being explained by changes in share that are offset by reciprocal changes in wine share. As for total consumption, only 3.6% of its variability is associated with the factor and overall only 4.1% of the variability in the entire data set is.

Before beginning the discussion of the factor analytic regressions, it is worth taking a moment to recap the three factor analyses. A three factor solution

Table 3.5
Factor Analysis of Share of Consumption and Total Consumption

		Beer (+) vs Liquor (−)	Total Consumption	Wine Share
Share	Beer	.98	− . 02	. 19
	Wine	. 54	. 40	.74
	Liquor	−. 90	− . 14	− . 41
	Total Consumption	. 03	.98	. 19
	Variance (%)	69 . 5	26 . 3	4 . 1
	Cum Variance (%)	69 . 5	95 . 9	100 . 0

characterizes the predictor data set. One factor is a linear trend including Year, Population, Income, and the two price variables. The remaining two factors describe advertising of wine and liquor combined and second beer. The factor analysis of the four consumption series results in a two factor solution, one factor consisting of beer, wine, and total consumption and the second, of liquor and total consumption. The last factor analysis of beverage category shares and total consumption reveals three dimensions, the first describing a trade-off in share between liquor and beer mostly and wine to a lesser degree, a total consumption factor and lastly a wine share dimension. The next step in the analysis is to relate the factors to one another in a regression context.

The results of the factor analytic regressions for consumption are given in Table 3.6. Before examining substantive results of the analysis it is valuable to note some of the special features of regression on factor scores. First and foremost, all variables listed in Table 3.6, both predictor and outcome, are independent and uncorrelated. As a result, the regression coefficients measure the unique relationship of each predictor factor to the consumption factor. Recall, however, that while the mutually exclusive contribution of each factor can be quantified, the factors themselves are composites of many influences. The unique contribution of each predictor variable can be assessed but only indirectly through its factor loading.

A second important feature of the analysis is that factor scores, both predictor and predicted, are normalized such that their mean is 0 and standard deviation is 1. The intercept in all equations is still the overall mean of the dependent variable, which is 0 in every case and has been omitted from all factor analytic regression tables as a result. Another implication of normalization is that the raw and standardized regression coefficients are identical and only one is given

Table 3.6
Factor Analytic Regressions for Consumption

	Beer, Wine & Total		Liquor & Total	
	b	t	b	t
Trend	.970	31.33*	−.093	−.97
Wine & Liquor Advertising	.159	5.13*	.729	7.59*
Beer Advertising	.018	.60	−.383	−3.99*
R^2		.967		.687
Adj R^2		.965		.659

*p < .05

in the tables. Nevertheless, the coefficient can be squared to obtain the percentage of variance in the dependent variable that is accounted for by the independent one, a procedure that makes even more sense given the predictors are uncorrelated.

Returning again then to Table 3.6 with these interpretative guidelines in mind, we can see that the beer, wine and total consumption factor is significantly related to the trend and wine and liquor advertising factors. With respect to the former, nearly all of the variability in beer, wine, and total consumption over time, 94.1%, can be attributed to the combined effects of population, prices and a linear trend. Squaring the coefficient for wine and liquor advertising we see that 2.5% of the variability in beer, wine, and total consumption is accounted by the advertising factor, a finding that is very consistent with past research. Beer advertising contributes trivially to the mix, accounting for a mere .03% of variability, a relationship that is, of course, not statistically significant.

For the second regression summarized in Table 3.6 it can be seen that liquor and total consumption is unrelated to the trend variable but is strongly influenced by advertising. Fully 53.1% of the variability in liquor and total consumption is associated with the variability in wine and liquor advertising, by far the strongest advertising relationship that has been seen in this or other studies. Beer advertising also seems to influence liquor and total consumption, as we might expect, in a negative manner. Thus the higher the amount of beer advertising the less the amount of liquor consumed. Overall the relationship for liquor and total consumption is weaker than that for beer, wine, and total consumption,

68.7% of the variability of the former is explained by the three regressor variables as compared with 96.7% of the latter.

The second factor analytic regression for share of consumption and total consumption is given in Table 3.7. The first factor regressed quantifies the trade-off between beer and liquor shares. Again, we see a significant trend factor, which in this case accounts for 35.5% of the variability in the beer-liquor trade-off. Beer share increases at the expense of liquor share, therefore, as a function of growth in the 20- to 34-year-old population, income declines in prices and as a simple function of time.

The share factor is also significantly and negatively related to wine and liquor advertising, suggesting that beer consumption gains share from liquor consumption when wine and liquor advertising are low. Nearly two-fifths (18.8%) of the beer-liquor share trade-off is attributable to wine and liquor advertising. Not surprisingly then, beer advertising is positively related to beer share gains from liquor although the result is not statistically significant and accounts only for 2.4% of the variability in the trade-off.

All three predictor factors are significantly related to the total consumption factor, and when taken simultaneously the three variables are associated with 87.0% of the variance in total consumption, 85.8% on an adjusted basis. As for individual predictors, the composite effects of time, income, prices, and population, labeled Trend, are positively related to total consumption, indicating that total consumption increased over time and with gains in income in the 20- to 34-year-old segment of the population and declines in prices. Trend effects accounted for 42.3% of the variance in total consumption.

Considering the advertising factors, both were related significantly with total consumption but their associations were directionally opposite. Wine and liquor advertising is positively associated with total consumption and accounts for 37% of the variability; beer advertising is much weaker with only 7.7% of the variability in total consumption explained by it. Further, the beer advertising relationship is negative, indicating that total consumption was high when beer advertising was low and vice versa. The opposite was true of wine and liquor advertising.

The last regression given in Table 3.7 is for the wine share factor. In this instance the relationship is weaker, $R^2 = .283$, and only one variable, Trend, is significantly related to wine share. Like total consumption gains in income, the 20- to 34-year-old population, declines in prices and time are related to increases in wine share, accounting for 17.9% of the variability. The two advertising factors are not significantly related to wine share and the signs of the regression coefficients are counterintuitive. Wine share is apparently negatively related to wine and liquor advertising but is positively related with beer advertising. Given the comparatively narrow range in which wine share varies over time, the results are probably not indicative of real relationships, despite the fact that the beer advertising coefficient approaches statistical significance. With respect to vari-

Table 3.7
Factor Analytic Regressions for Share of Consumption and Total Consumption

	Beer (+) vs Liquor (−)		Total Consumption		Wine Share	
	b	t	b	t	b	t
Trend	.596	5.29*	.650	10.51*	.423	2.91*
Wine & Liquor Advertising	−.434	−3.85*	.608	9.83*	−.150	−1.04
Beer Advertising	.155	1.37	−.278	−4.49*	.284	1.96
R^2	.568		.870		.283	
Adj R^2	.530		.858		.219	

*$p < .05$

ance explained, the wine and liquor advertising and beer advertising factors only account for 2.3% and 8.1% in wine share, respectively.

It is worth taking a moment to summarize the findings from the factor analytic regressions. With respect to consumption roughly two-thirds (65.6%) of the variance in total consumption is associated with beer and wine consumption, as shown in the first factor in Table 3.4, and approximately a third (33.6%) is related to liquor consumption. As shown in Table 3.6, wine and liquor advertising is significantly related to both consumption factors accounting for 2.5% of the variability in beer, wine, and total consumption and a much larger share, 53.1%, of the variance in liquor and total consumption. Beer advertising, perhaps surprisingly, does not significantly correlate with beer, wine, and total consumption but is negatively and significantly related to liquor and total consumption, accounting for 14.7% of the variability in the factor.

Considering beverage shares and total consumption, Table 3.5 indicates that total consumption is largely independent of shifts in share across beverage categories. For instance, the factor that represents the give-and-take between beer and liquor shares accounts for a near trivial .09% of the variance in total consumption, while the wine share factor explains little more, 3.6%. As for the regression analysis (Table 3.7), the relationship between advertising and beer-liquor share fluctuations is straightforward. Beer share increases at the expense of liquor share when beer advertising increases or when wine and liquor advertising decreases. With respect to wine share, advertising relationships are not significant and the signs of the coefficients are directionally reversed from what might be expected.

Looking at the last regression analysis, both advertising factors are significantly related to total consumption and the results in Table 3.7 are consistent with those in Table 3.6. That is, wine and liquor advertising is positively related to total consumption and beer advertising is negatively related. Total consumption is higher when wine and liquor advertising is relatively elevated and when beer advertising tends to be low. The magnitude of the coefficients suggests that the wine and liquor advertising relationship is the stronger of the two accounting for nearly five times more of the variance in total consumption, 37.7% versus 7.7%.

SUPPLEMENTARY ANALYSES

As noted earlier, there are several limitations in the data and techniques used in this chapter. Specifically, the specification for advertising is constrained to magazine spending or pages, the only advertising measures that were available for the entire duration of the study. The lack of other advertising data complicates the discussion, given the widely disproportionate amounts of total advertising budgets that are committed to magazines for the three beverage types. And from a statistical viewpoint, the regression analyses are simply correlational and no temporal causality is assumed.

In an attempt to overcome these potential shortcomings, several supplementary analyses were performed. Initially, we will consider alternative specifications of the advertising variable. In particular, the standard demand models were rerun using Magazine Pages, Total 6 Media, and Total Media, and the results for both consumption and share of consumption are given in this section. Clearly, the best specification for advertising is Total Media and secondly Total 6 Media. However, these data are available only for 1970 and thereafter so any relationships seen may be a function of just the abbreviated time series and could disappear if data had been available for the full time period.

To investigate the issue of temporal ordering in the data and thereby strengthen our conclusions about advertising, a series of time-series analyses were performed. The advertising series were crosscorrelated with the consumption and share of consumption data and the coefficients were examined for lead and lag structure.

Considering first the various specifications for advertising, Table 3.8 provides the relationships with consumption and Table 3.9 with share of consumption. In the tables we have chosen not to display the entire regression model for each advertising specification but rather to present just the unstandardized regression coefficient and associated test of significance. In the tables, Magazine Ad $ is identical to the specification and results given in Tables 3.1 and 3.2, while Magazine Pages is simply the number of pages of advertising for each beverage category each year and Total 6 Media and Total Media are expressed in millions of dollars deflated to 1982 levels.[4]

Returning to Table 3.8 for consumption, it can be seen that advertising is not significantly related to beer consumption regardless of the specification used. Moreover, all the signs of the coefficients are negative, suggesting that the contemporaneous relationship of beer advertising with beer consumption is counterintuitive; beer consumption is low when beer advertising is high and vice versa. The relationship between liquor consumption and liquor advertising is direct. That is, when liquor advertising is high, liquor consumption is as well. Further, this relationship was statistically significant over the 38-year time period, but was not for the shorter series of 20 years for Total 6 Media and Total Media. Finally, for wine consumption the advertising relationships change radically, depending on the length of time studied and the specification of advertising. In the longer series where only magazine advertising is considered, the relationship between consumption and advertising is negative and not statistically significant. When more media types are investigated over a shorter time period, the relationship is positive and statistically significant.

The pattern of relationships between advertising and share of consumption is quite similar with the only changes involving beer share. In this instance, beer advertising is positively associated with three of the four advertising specifications but not significantly in any case. Liquor share is again directly related to liquor advertising and the association is statistically significant in the longer series using magazine advertising indicators. Wine share, as before, is negatively

Table 3.8
Regression Coefficients for Different Advertising Specifications with Consumption

	Beer		Wine		Liquor	
	b	t	b	t	b	t
Magazine Ad $	-.020	-.24	-.112	-.68	.150	4.00*
Magazine Pages	-.000035	-.73	-.000038	-.82	.000046	2.68*
Total 6 Media	-.0000113	-1.99	.00163	3.30*	.00000611	.67
Total Media	-.0000109	-1.45	.0000415	3.15*	.000000542	.60

*p < .05

Table 3.9
Regression Coefficients for Different Advertising Specifications with Share of Consumption

	Beer		Wine		Liquor	
	b	t	b	t	b	t
Magazine Ad $	−1.150	−.24	−6.010	−.95	3.078	4.36*
Magazine Pages	.0017	.63	−.0011	−.62	.0010	2.90*
Total 6 Media	.0000532	.37	.0000423	3.25*	.0000343	.17
Total Media	.0000782	.51	.00160	3.21*	.0000238	.12

*p < .05

related to the two magazine advertising measures over 27 years, albeit no nificantly so. The relationship becomes positive and significant when a broader definition of advertising is used over a shorter time period.

For share data, 9 of the 12 relationships are positive as are the four statistically significant ones. Thus, when advertising has a meaningful relationship with beverage share more advertising tends to be associated with higher shares regardless of beverage type. The same conclusion holds for consumption where again the only statistically significant relationships are positive and hence higher levels of advertising for a beverage type are associated with higher levels of consumption for it. Nevertheless, given the lack of consistent positive and statistically significant findings, especially in raw data time series in which even the most minor relationships should be significant, we must question the overall power of advertising to influence category consumption or share.

The last analyses to be considered are presented in Tables 3.10 and 3.11, respectively the crosscorrelations of advertising with consumption and share of consumption. Crosscorrelations permit us to examine time dependent relationships in the data by offsetting time measurements that are used to calculate the correlation coefficients. The correlations in the rows labeled -1 and -2 measure the extent of the relationships when advertising precedes consumption or share which, in turn, are said to lag advertising by one or two years. Conversely, correlations in rows labeled 1 and 2 relate consumption and share to advertising when the former precede the latter. Row 0 gives the correlation when advertising, consumption, and share of consumption are measured in the same year.

The study data set permits crosscorrelations up to lag -12 and lead 12, such that advertising could be associated with consumption and share of consumption as much as 12 years prior to the spending or 12 years after it. We have chosen to report just 5 of the 25 possible crosscorrelations, contemporaneous, two leads and two lags. A number of previous studies (Ackoff and Emshoff, 1975; Assmus et al., 1984; Clarke, 1976; Peles, 1969, 1971a, 1971b) investigated the duration of advertising effects for alcoholic beverage products and found that any effects that are noticeable are fully depreciated within two years. We concluded therefore that any significant crosscorrelations with lags greater than 2 were more apt to be spurious than real and we did not report or interpret them.

On the other hand, if we assume a priori that advertising affects demand, one might wonder why crosscorrelations where consumption or share precede advertising are of interest, that is, why leads are reported at all. Again the econometric literature offers a rationale. When examining time dependent relationships several researchers (Duffy, 1990; Grabowski, 1976; Smith, 1988) found that while there were no important contemporaneous or lagged relationships, significant correlations were in evidence when demand led advertising. From this the authors concluded that marketers set advertising spending levels in a budgetary context in reference to past sales. Past sales of a product are used to predict future revenue and hence how much a company can afford to spend advertising a product. To investigate this possibility we have calculated cross-

Table 3.10
Crosscorrelations of Consumption with Advertising

	Time Difference (Years)	Beer	CONSUMPTION Wine	Liquor
Lead	2	−.23	.21	.33*
	1	−.14	.39*	.13
	0	−.07	−.11	.17
Lag	−1	−.17	.07	.06
	−2	−.12	−.08	.02

*p < .05

Table 3.11

Crosscorrelations of Share of Consumption with Advertising

SHARE OF CONSUMPTION

Time Difference (Years)	Beer	Wine	Liquor
Lead			
2	−.17	.11	.19
1	−.08	.26	.01
0	.04	−.20	.04
Lag			
1	−.10	−.01	.08
2	.08	−.11	.03

correlations when consumption and share of consumption precede advertising. But as before, we have assumed that any budgetary effect is almost certainly not longer than two years and have only chosen to report and interpret up to two leads.

The crosscorrelations of consumption with advertising are shown in Table 3.10. No contemporaneous or lagged correlation for any of the three beverage products is statistically significant. From these statistics it is probably safe to conclude that magazine advertising spending has little impact on consumption of any of the three types of alcoholic products. We do, however, see two significant leading crosscorrelations, at one year for wine and two years for liquor. Like other researchers we see some support for the notion that advertising levels are set in a budgetary context with respect to past sales.

The findings reported in Table 3.11 indicate that there is no significant cross-correlations, contemporaneous, lead or lag for any of the three product category shares with advertising. This lack of any significant relationships for share of consumption and magazine advertising spending is again curious given the expectation that advertising is more apt to affect shares than primary demand. However, these results may suggest that if advertising affects share it would be at the individual product or brand level and not at the level of beverage category.

SUMMARY

In this chapter we have investigated the relationship between advertising and consumption of alcohol in a number of ways. Initially, we examined a simple demand specification for consumption and share of consumption that included advertising in a model with a trend factor and demographic and economic variables. Next we removed multicollinearity from the predictors and included total consumption in the analysis by finding the factor structure in the predictor and outcome variables and subsequently relating the structural dimensions in a series of regression analyses using factor scores as input. The last stage involved the exploration for media effects when different specifications of advertising were used and when time dependent relationships in the data set were examined.

As expected, demand for alcoholic beverages as well as share of consumption was strongly influenced by economic and demographic trends. Increases in the population of 20- to 34-year-olds were associated with gains in consumption and share for beer and wine but with reciprocal losses for liquor share and alcohol consumption from liquor drinking. Generally, price was negatively related to consumption of beer and liquor but unrelated to wine demand, while increased consumer affluence was associated with greater consumption of beer and liquor but again did not impact wine demand. When share of consumption was considered, rising personal income increased liquor consumption at the expense of beer drinking. The opposite relationship was true of price such that beer consumption was elevated when prices were high relative to the CPI but share shifted to liquor when relative prices were low.

The primary demand models offer some but not terribly strong support for a relationship between advertising and alcohol consumption. No statistically significant association was found between magazine advertising spending and consumption or share of consumption for beer or wine products. Liquor consumption and share, by comparison, were significantly and directly related to advertising spending in magazines with higher levels of advertising associated with higher levels of liquor consumption and liquor share of total consumption.

From the coefficient in the demand model we estimate that an additional $1 million of real advertising spending in magazines for liquor products is associated with an increase in alcohol consumption of .15 gallons or 19.2 ounces of raw alcohol consumption per adult per year from liquor drinking. This is roughly equivalent to one additional shot of distilled spirits per adult every three weeks. As always, we must caution that this figure assumes that all other factors are held constant and recall that the association is a correlational not causal one. Increases in alcohol consumption from liquor might also come at the expense of alcohol ingestion from another source if beer and wine are substitutes for liquor such that the net impact on total consumption could be minimal.

The issue of total consumption and advertising was taken up in factor analytic regressions. The preliminary factor analyses revealed that approximately two-thirds of the variability in total consumption was associated with beer and wine consumption and one-third was related to liquor consumption. Regression on factor scores subsequently indicated that beer, wine, and a portion of total consumption were positively related to wine and liquor advertising. Liquor consumption and its fraction of total consumption meanwhile were positively related to wine and liquor advertising as well. However, the liquor and total consumption factor was negatively related to beer advertising, suggesting that liquor and the associated fractional component of total consumption were low when beer advertising was high.

The regression analysis using share factors was also insightful. When share of consumption and total consumption were factor analyzed, it was found that nearly seven-tenths of the variability in share shifts involved a direct give-and-take between beer and liquor products. Wine share moved independently of this primary share dynamic as did total consumption. In fact, total consumption was unrelated to the share of any alcoholic beverage category, implying that absolute alcohol consumption is unaffected by source of consumption. Thus, beer and liquor products appear to be substitutes, wine share follows its own course, and total consumption is largely unaffected by share shifts.

When the share of consumption and total consumption factors were regressed on the demand factors, wine and liquor advertising was found to be negatively related to the beer-liquor trade-off factor; that is, beer tends to gain share at the expense of liquor when wine and liquor advertising is low and liquor share is high relative to beer when wine and liquor advertising is higher. Wine share was unrelated to advertising. Total consumption, finally, was positively associated with wine and liquor advertising but negatively related to beer magazine advertising spending. High levels of advertising would be associated with high levels of total consumption if the advertising were for wine and liquor products, therefore, but the opposite would be true if the advertising were for beer products.

Using deflated magazine advertising spending as an indicator of advertising intensity was a necessary evil given the vagaries of media data collection. However, the specification could have introduced some bias given the substantially different proportions of total media spending for the three beverage types accounted for by magazine advertising, approximately 70%, 12%, and 4% for liquor, wine, and beer products in that order. It is possible that the reason a significant advertising relationship was found only for liquor consumption is the way advertising was measured, in terms of deflated magazine advertising spending. Stated differently, advertising might be related to beer and wine consumption if other media were considered.

To investigate this possibility the demand models were rerun with different advertising measures. The inclusion of magazine advertising pages did not alter the substantive findings; liquor consumption was still significantly related to advertising over the four decade study period and wine and beer consumption were not. Using total media spending and total spending in six major media limited the scope of the analysis to 21 years, 1970–1990. Beer consumption remained unrelated to advertising, while contradictory findings were obtained from the other two beverage categories. Liquor was not significantly related to advertising over the shorter series, whereas there was a positive relationship between wine advertising and wine consumption over the last two decades. The findings are mixed, the only consistent finding being the lack of a significant relationship between beer consumption and beer advertising.

As noted earlier, the results given in this chapter are correlational in nature; they are indicative of a relationship not effects. Causality would be more certain if time dependent relationships were evident in the data and to assess this possibility, a series of crosscorrelations with leads and lags were computed. In no instance, for any beverage category, was a significant crosscorrelation observed when advertising was contemporaneous with or preceded consumption or share of consumption. These findings may be the strongest argument presented in this chapter that advertising does not affect category consumption or share, again recognizing the caveat that only advertising spending in magazines was considered.

We did, however, observe several significant relationships when consumption preceded advertising. This seemingly illogical finding does have a rational foundation and has been reported on a number of occasions by other investigators. It has been suggested that marketers set advertising spending targets in a budgetary context. They estimate current sales based on past performance and use the figure to determine how much advertising can be afforded. Past product sales and consumption become then a determinant of future advertising spending. Our data suggest that this mechanism may be operative one year ahead for wine and two years ahead for liquor products.

Taking the findings as a whole, we can find no strong or consistent pattern of advertising relationships. Beer consumption is unrelated to advertising regardless of specification, time period, or time order. Wine and liquor consumption are related to advertising in some analyses but the results are not consistent across time periods and advertising specifications and disappear entirely when time-ordered analyses are conducted. Total consumption does appear to be related to advertising of wine and liquor products but negatively related to beer advertising. Again, the pattern is not uniform.

We might expect the strongest relationships to be present in the raw data time series. The fact that few relationships were found and the ones that were did not appear consistently argues against a large or meaningful contribution of advertising to beverage category or total consumption. In the next chapter we will investigate whether even these limited advertising relationships continue to be evident when the data are more tightly defined.

Chapter 4

Changes in Alcohol Consumption

In the preceding chapter we examined the relationship between advertising and alcohol consumption and share of consumption. More generally, the factors that influence demand for various alcohol products and alcohol consumption as well as share of consumption between beverage types were identified. The fundamental nature of this analysis was to correlate trends in demand determinants and advertising with contemporaneous trends in consumption and share of consumption. Thus, we were able to ascertain how the various predictors, advertising, and consumption time series were moving relative to each other over the four decades studied.

While this type of analysis is useful in spotting gross patterns in the data and in revealing broad structural relationships, it does have distinct limitations. Because data are measured over a comparatively brief period, correlations tend to be artificially inflated leading to multicollinearity among predictors and potentially overstated relationships between predictor and outcome variables. Consequently, while the analyses of the untransformed or raw data provide valuable insight into the trends over time, definitive conclusions about the strength of any advertising relationships should be considered in the context of a full range of analytic options, including time series methods and data transformations.

One such data transformation is to remove the nonstationary aspects of the data, that is, the gross trends, by calculating first differences. In this method, the observed value of any variable at one point in time, t_0, is adjusted by subtracting its value at the immediately preceding time point, t_{-1}. By taking first differences we are examining the change in data over time such that the yearly change in a predictor, say income, is correlated with the contemporaneous yearly change in an outcome variable, like beer consumption.

Analyzing first differences in essence moves the focus of the study away from the full time series and its trend to the margin of the distribution; in other words, only that portion of time series that varies from year to year. First differences tend, therefore, to be less influenced by major societal and macroeconomic forces that are manifest over many years and even decades and instead are only affected by short-term phenomena whose duration is a year or less. As a consequence, when the change in a predictor variable is consistently related to a change in an outcome there are fewer possible spurious causes for the observed association and the result is much more likely to be indicative of a "real" relationship, the influence of other factors having been removed by taking first differences.

In this chapter then the original time series data will be differenced and the relationships between the yearly change in demand predictors, advertising, alcohol consumption, and share of consumption will be examined. The structure of the chapter parallels exactly that of Chapter 3. Initially we will look at the standard demand models for consumption and share of consumption. Next, the predictor and outcome data sets will be factor analyzed, not so much in this case to remove multicollinearity, which tends to be minimal in differenced series but rather to combine total consumption with consumption of other beverage types and share of consumption. The last section of the chapter reports the results of the two supplementary analyses using different advertising specifications and time series techniques.

CONSUMPTION

The results of the three demand models for beer, wine, and liquor consumption differences are presented in Table 4.1. The effect of taking first differences is immediately apparent in the findings. First, far fewer of the predictor variables are significantly related to consumption, suggesting, as implied above, that there are fewer "real" relationships present in the data. Second, the R^2 and adjusted R^2 statistics are greatly reduced from the preceding analysis. Whereas the analyses in Chapter 3 were influenced by the nonstationary, monotonic trends in the data producing large correlations over time, the differenced data removes the trends and concentrates on the essential features of the analysis.

There are several other somewhat more technical considerations to keep in mind when reviewing the results. As before, the regression models have been centered and the intercept term measures the average annual change in per capita consumption for each of the three beverage types. Note, as an example, that the intercept term, b_0, in the beer consumption model is .009 and that this result is statistically significant. Interpreting the coefficient we can conclude that beer consumption increased on average by .009 gallons for every person in the country 15 years or older every year of the study period. So over the 38 years studied, annual adult per capita consumption of alcohol from beer drinking should have increased by .34 gallons (.009 $\times$ 38).

The remaining raw or unstandardized coefficients, bs, in the table can be inter-

Table 4.1
Regression Models for Change in Consumption

		Beer			Wine			Liquor		
		b	beta	t	b	beta	t	b	beta	t
Year		−.0002	−.078	−.52	−.0003	−.133	−.52	−.002	−.601	−4.81*
Population		.015	.536	3.17*	.006	.322	1.23	−.005	−.148	−.82
Income		.0004	.044	.29	−.00008	−.016	−.08	.004	.345	2.41*
Price Index	Beer	−.147	−.126	−.77						
	Wine				.107	.152	.76			
	Liquor							−.362	−.463	−2.32*
Magazine Ad \$	Beer	.050	.113	.76						
	Wine				−.149	−.296	−1.52			
	Liquor							.020	.145	1.15
b_0		.009		2.69*	.004		1.34	.001		.19
R^2			.334			.301			.552	
Adj R^2			.226			.127			.479	

*$p < .05$

preted in a similar manner. Each measures the change in average annual adult per capita consumption that would result from a unit change in a predictor variable. Again, looking at the beer consumption model results, the unstandardized coefficient for Income is .0004 suggesting that alcohol intake from beer consumption increases by .0004 gallons per adult for every $10 additional personal disposal income an American adult receives.

The coefficient for Year takes on a quite different interpretation in the first difference model. Previously it measured the average annual change in consumption. In the models in Table 4.1 the linear trend has been removed by first differencing and the average annual change in consumption is quantified by the intercept term. In the first difference model Year measures the quadratic trend in the data and is akin to measuring the acceleration or change in velocity of the first differences. Put another way, Year measures whether the rate of change in the data is increasing or decreasing significantly over time.

The last item of note in Table 4.1 are the columns of standardized coefficients or betas. These statistics were omitted from the tables in Chapter 3 because multicollinearity among the predictors made them effectively meaningless. With this problem eliminated by differencing the coefficients have interpretative value. Specifically, the coefficients measure the strength of each relationship on a common scale so the predictors can be directly compared. Further, it is possible to square the standardized coefficient to determine the amount of variance, in percentage terms, in the dependent variable that is accounted for. or "explained" by each independent variable.

With this as background, the substantive results in Table 4.1 can now be discussed. For beer consumption we can see that only two relationships are statistically significant. As noted before, the intercept term in the model is significantly different from zero, indicating that alcohol ingestion from beer drinking has grown steadily over time. The only other significant relationship is for Population. The unstandardized coefficient reveals that alcohol consumption via beer increases on average by .015 gallons per adult for every additional 1 million 20- to 34-year-olds in the population. Moreover, the unstandardized coefficient, .536, when squared shows that fully 28.7% of the variability in beer alcohol consumption is accounted for by population changes.

As for the remaining predictors, the classic demand influences of Income and Price work as expected, positive and negative, respectively, but neither approaches statistical significance and in order account for only .0016% and 1.6% of the variability in beer alcohol consumption differences. Advertising likewise has only a minor impact on change in beer consumption. For every annual change equaling an additional 1 million constant dollars of magazine advertising spending alcohol consumption from beer drinking will change by .05 gallons per adult. This relationship explains just 1.3% of the variability in consumption—a finding that is quite consistent with survey-based correlational studies. Overall changes in the predictor variables explain 33.4% of the variability in changes in per capita alcohol consumption sourced from beer drinking and only 22.6% on an adjusted basis.

Wine consumption is quite stable over time with only minor changes being evidenced over the study period. This fact is expressed clearly in the regression results. The intercept term suggests that wine consumption has increased over time but not significantly so. Further, none of the other regression coefficients are statistically significant. And finally, the amount of variance in wine drinking explained by the demand model is comparatively small, 30.1% and only 12.7% when adjusted for the length of the series.

With respect to the individual predictors, changes in alcohol consumption from wine drinking are positively related to changes in the young adult population, increasing .006 gallons per capita for each extra 1 million 20- to 34-year-olds in the population. The signs of the classic demand predictors are reversed from what would be forecast by theory, but given the results are not statistically significant this is not too worrisome. Another counterintuitive finding is seen for advertising for which a positive change in magazine advertising spending for wine products is associated with a negative change in alcohol consumption per capita from wine drinking. The advertising effect is fairly strong on a percentage variance explained basis, 8.8%, but is not significantly different from zero. Finally, there appears to be nc meaningful pattern in the rate of change of wine consumption as indicated by the lack of significant findings for Year.

Considerably more is going on in the first difference liquor consumption demand model, the predictors in this instance accounting for 55.2% of the variability in liquor alcohol consumption differences and 47.9% on an adjusted basis. Although the intercept suggests that on average the change in alcohol consumed via liquor products in near zero, .001 gallons to be precise, the coefficient for Year is negative and significant. This finding indicates that the liquor alcohol consumption is declining at an accelerating rate over time, a fact that can be seen visually in the last 15 years of data in Figure 2.7.

As has been seen before, liquor consumption seems to be particularly susceptible to classic demand determinants. Both Income and Price are significant and the signs of the coefficients are as one would expect based on economic theory. Changes in alcohol ingestion sourced from liquor consumption increase .004 gallons per adult per year on average for each positive difference of ten constant dollars of disposable personal income Americans have and decreases -.362 gallons when change in the liquor price index doubles relative to the CPI.

Magazine advertising differences are positively associated with changes in liquor consumption but not significantly so. The raw coefficient for Magazine Ad $ suggests that for a plus change of one million dollars in liquor advertising spending, alcohol consumption will change by an additional .02 gallons per adult per year. The standardized coefficient indicates that 2.1% of the variability in alcohol consumption from liquor drinking is accounted for by magazine advertising expenditures. Again, the variance explained figure is in line with the relationship observed in other studies.

To summarize broadly the results of the three regression models given in Table 4.1 then, it would appear that alcohol consumption from beer drinking increases significantly year over year, while liquor drinking declines at an accelerating rate over time and wine consumption is largely unchanged. Beer drinking is driven primarily by demographics and liquor consumption is influenced most by economic factors, consumer affluence, and product prices. Wine consumption, by contrast, is unaffected by demand determinants since it changes little over time. These patterns are captured in the adjusted R^2 statistic, which suggests that roughly a quarter, an eighth, and about a half of the variability in beer, wine, and liquor consumption differences are explained by changes in the demand variables.

More germane to the central focus of the study, in no case is advertising significantly related to consumption. In two instances, beer and liquor, the relationship is positive but the variance explained is only in the 1 to 2% range. Advertising explains a much greater proportion of the variance in wine consumption, 8.8%, but the relationship is the opposite of what one would expect, a positive change in magazine advertising spending for wine products being associated with a negative change in wine consumption and vice versa. Taken as a whole these results do not suggest a large role for advertising in determining alcohol consumption.

SHARE OF CONSUMPTION

The regression models for change in share of consumption for the three beverage types are given in Table 4.2. Again, keep in mind that the unstandardized regression coefficients quantify the change in share of a particular beverage with the unit change in the predictor variable. For the beer model a change in the population of 20- to 34-year-olds by 1 million would lead to a positive change in beer share of .057 points. The betas or standardized coefficients again measure the strength of the relationship between differences in predictor variables and consumption on a common scale and as before, the coefficient can be squared to obtain the amount of variance in the dependent variable changes that are explained or accounted for by changes in a particular independent one.

Another interesting feature of the analysis is that by expressing consumption for a beverage type as a share of total consumption we have created a sum-zero game; that is, a gain in share by one beverage type must be reflected as a loss of share in some combination of the others. This trade-off is most obvious and direct when the same predictor variable such as Population or Income appear in all models. It is less apparent when a term like Price or Magazine Ad $ is specific to a beverage type and present in only one model. Nevertheless, the analyses are sufficiently interlaced to make it prudent to discuss the results in concert.

A good illustration of this point is the three intercept terms. Each measures the average annual change in share of consumption such that beer share increases

Table 4.2
Regression Models for Change in Share of Consumption

	Beer			Wine			Liquor		
	b	beta	t	b	beta	t	b	beta	t
Year	.038	.629	5.01*	.010	.159	.58	−.034	−.551	−4.84*
Population	.057	.070	.49	.232	.365	1.29	−.455	−.542	−3.30*
Income	−.038	−.161	−1.26	.013	.083	.36	.073	.304	2.33*
Price Index — Beer	−5.598	−.164	−1.20						
Price Index — Wine				2.077	.092	.42			
Price Index — Liquor							−7.711	−.421	−2.32*
Magazine Ad $ — Beer	−.328	−.025	−.20						
Magazine Ad $ — Wine				−4.592	−.285	−1.36			
Magazine Ad $ — Liquor							.351	.106	.93
b_0	.080		1.01	.104		1.09	−.175		−2.44*
R^2		.534			.186			.629	
Adj R^2		.458			−.018			.569	

*$p < .05$

by .08 points per year and wine by .104 points. These gains are offset almost exactly by share losses in liquor consumption which fell .175 points per year on average. In fact, if the three shares were measured over the same time period, the intercept terms would sum to zero. They do not simply because the wine series is 11 years shorter.

Taking the results in Table 4.2 as a system then, it can be seen that the demographic surge of maturing baby-boomers that swelled the 20- to 34-year-old age group over the 38 years studied is associated with positive changes in beer and wine shares of total consumption and negative changes in liquor shares. In fact, each additional 1 million 20- to 34-year-olds in the population is associated with an increase in the average change of share for beer of .057 points and .232 share points for wine over and above its average annual change. While neither of these relationships is statistically significant, the reciprocal impact on change in liquor share is. The addition of each new 1 million 20- to 34-year-olds to the population accelerates the average loss of liquor share by .455 points and again had the series been equal length this figure would have exactly offset the combined beer and wine gains. Looked at in another way, population shifts accounted for 29.4% of the variability in liquor share changes, 13.3% of wine share changes and just .5% of the variability in beer share differences.

Income also has a significant association with changes in liquor share this time in a positive direction. That is, the average annual change in liquor share increases by .073 points for each positive change of $10 in real personal disposable income and this effect accounts for 9.2% of the differences in liquor share. Wine share also benefits from increasing consumer affluence but to a much lesser degree. A plus change of $10 in personal disposable income is associated with a gain of .013 wine share points, an association that is not statistically significant and explains less than a percent (.7%) of the variance in wine share shifts. Beer share changes absorb the affluence-related positive differences seen for wine and liquor. While not significant, positive changes in personal disposable income are associated with negative ones in beer share, $10 gained in wealth equating to a loss in share of .038 points.

Price changes have a large impact on share shifts particularly for liquor share. In this instance, if the price of liquor were to change positively by the size of the CPI, that is, if the liquor to CPI ratio moved from 1.2 to 2.2, liquor share of total consumption would drop 7.7 points. A similar drop would be seen for beer share of 5.6 share points. Surprisingly, wine share changes are directly associated with changes in relative price, with share estimated to increase 2.1 points for a doubling in relative price. Perhaps fortunately, this finding does not approach statistical significance, allowing us to avoid a difficult interpretation. Overall the importance of the price differences to share changes can be seen by the percentage of variance explained, 17.7% for liquor share changes 2.7% and .8% for beer and wine share changes, respectively.

There is no statistically significant relationship between changes in magazine advertising spending of any category of alcoholic beverage product and its change in share. Quite the contrary in two instances, beer and wine, positive changes in magazine advertising spending are associated with negative changes in share. Only for liquor share are positive differences in advertising associated with positive share gains. The amount of variance explained by advertising differences ranges from .06% for beer share changes to 8.1% for wine share differences, liquor share shifts being intermediate at 1.1%.

There are two remaining points to mention before drawing conclusions from the analyses reported in Table 4.2. First are the coefficients for Year, two of which are statistically significant. The rate of change for beer share is increasing by .038 points per year, which accounts for 39.6% of the variability in the differences over almost 40 years. This accelerating shift to beer consumption comes at the expense of liquor share which declines as a percentage of total consumption at an accelerating rate. The growing speed with which liquor share shifts to beer share accounts for 30.4% of the variability in liquor share differences over time. Meanwhile, wine share changes are largely independent of this beer-liquor share tug-of-war. Only 2.5% of the variability in wine share shifts are explained by the rate of change variable Year.

This primary dynamic present in the data is corroborated by the explanatory power of the three regression models. Liquor and beer share changes appear to be strongly influenced by the changes in the demand determinants. Over half of the variability in beer share changes are explained by the model, $R^2 = .534$, and 45.8% on an adjusted basis. The effect is even stronger for liquor share differences with 62.9% of the variability accounted for by the model and 56.9% on an adjusted basis. Wine share changes, which again stand largely to the side of the share war between liquor and beer, are not strongly affected by the demand variables, 18.6% of the variance explained, and there is no apparent relationship when the data are adjusted for the length of the series, adjusted $R^2 = -.018$.

To recap the results of the regression analyses for changes in share of consumption, it would appear that the primary driving mechanism is a trade-off between beer and liquor share. This shift of total consumption to beer and away from liquor accelerates across the study period. Liquor share differences additionally are directly associated with positive changes in consumer affluence and inversely related to growth in the young adult segment of the population and increasing prices in relation to the CPI. As we have seen before, liquor share differences seem to be driven by both demographic and economic forces.

The paucity of significant findings for advertising is something of a puzzle. While the ability of advertising to build primary demand and thereby increase total alcohol consumption may be in doubt, its ability to shift sales from one brand to another rarely has been questioned. We might have expected then that changes in advertising spending for the three beverage types would have been associated with positive share shifts. Such is not the case, however, since in two instances the relationship is negative and in no case is it statistically significant. Perhaps the lack of any strong association is a function of the advertising specification, an issue that will be considered later in the chapter. Or perhaps, advertising differences do not affect category consumption shifts, but still operate at the level of individual brands.

FACTOR ANALYTIC REGRESSION

Table 4.3 presents the results of the factor analysis of the demand variables using differenced data. Note that as in Chapter 3, wine price index changes have been omitted to increase the number of years that can be included in the analysis. Also Magazine Pages has been included as a second indication of advertising intensity for each of the three beverage categories.

As shown in Table 4.3, a seven factor solution describes the data quite satisfactorily, explaining 95.4% of the variability in the demand variable differences. Further, the solution indicates that very little multicollinearity was present in the differenced series. Had there been a great deal of overlap in the information supplied by the independent variables the same variability in the predictor variables could have been explained by fewer factors and several variables would have loaded on each factor. As it is, the original variables for the most part each define a single factor. The exceptions to this are the two advertising measures which load on a factor for each beverage type and a factor that combines changes in the young adult population and relative liquor prices.

Looking at the individual factors, the strongest one accounting for nearly a quarter (24.8%) of the variability in differences represents beer advertising. It is followed in turn by liquor and wine advertising factors, accounting for 21.8% and 17.1% of the variance in the demand determinant differences. Taken as a unit, the three advertising factors explain nearly two-thirds or 63.7% of the variability in the differenced data.

As noted earlier, a fourth factor combines the changes in demographics and relative liquor prices and the composite variable explains 11.7% of the variance in the data set. Changes in personal disposable income are summarized by a single factor as are yearly differences in relative beer prices, the variance attributable to the factors is 8.7% and 5.0%, respectively. The final factor measures trend, which in a first difference data set is the quadratic term measuring the rate of change in the differences, and this factor explains 6.3% of the variability in the data set.

The second factor analysis of changes in consumption for beverage types and total is given in Table 4.4. A three factor solution reexpresses the original data set along orthogonal lines and by definition explains all of the variability in consumption differences. The first factor, explaining 61.5% of the variance, involves liquor consumption differences, while the second represents beer and the last wine. The last two factors account for 23.1% and 15.5% of the variance in the original data set.

The loadings for change in total consumption on the three factors is quite interesting. Total consumption differences correlated with a loading of .74 on the liquor change factor. This finding suggests that just over half of the differ-

Table 4.3
Factor Analysis of Change in Demand Predictors

		Beer Ads	Liquor Ads	Wine Ads	Population & Liquor Price	Income	Trend	Beer Price
Year		.05	-.10	-.11	.10	-.02	**.98**	-.06
Population		.03	-.01	-.06	**.96**	-.01	.09	-.14
Income		-.10	.07	.06	-.20	**.96**	-.02	.01
Price Index	Beer	.09	-.12	-.03	-.29	.02	-.06	**.94**
	Liquor	.09	-.07	-.07	**-.80**	.41	-.05	.22
Magazine Ad $	Beer	**.94**	.04	.20	-.10	-.05	.01	.03
	Wine	.33	.05	**.90**	-.04	.07	-.11	-.02
	Liquor	.10	**.96**	.10	-.08	.09	-.10	-.03
Magazine Pages	Beer	**.96**	.06	.06	.06	-.05	.04	.07
	Wine	.00	.17	**.96**	.03	-.01	-.03	-.02
	Liquor	.01	**.96**	.12	.12	-.02	-.01	-.10
Variance (%)		24.8	21.8	17.1	11.7	8.7	6.3	5.0
Cum Variance (%)		24.8	46.6	63.7	75.4	84.1	90.4	95.4

Table 4.4
Factor Analysis of Change in Consumption

	Liquor & Total	Beer & Total	Wine & Total
Beer	. 21	.98	. 03
Wine	. 11	. 06	.99
Liquor	.98	. 16	. 06
Total	. 74	. 59	. 33
Variance (%)	61 . 5	23 . 1	15 . 5
Cum Variance (%)	61 . 5	84 . 5	100 . 0

ences in total consumption, 54.8%, are attributable to changes in liquor consumption. The loading of .59 on the beer change factor indicates that 34.8% of the changes in total consumption are due to changes in beer drinking. The remaining variance, 10.9%, in total consumption differences is associated with changes in wine consumption.

The final factor analysis including change in total consumption with changes in share of consumption for the three beverage categories is given in Table 4.5. As presaged in the demand models for change in share of consumption (Table 4.2), one factor measures the tit-for-tat shifts in share between beer and liquor consumption. Beer share differences have a correlation of .93 with the factor and liquor share differences have a near equal opposite correlation of -.91. Moreover, the beer-liquor share trade-off accounts for half of all share differences, 49.8% to be precise. Wine share changes as suggested earlier stand apart and hence comprise a factor in their own right, accounting for 31.0% of the variability in the differenced data set.

Perhaps the most interesting aspect of the factor analysis is that changes in total consumption are almost completely unrelated to shifts in share or changes in the composition of consumption. Total consumption differences load on their own factor, which accounts for 96% of the variability in total consumption differences. The remaining variability in total consumption changes is attributable to the beer-liquor trade-off factor, 3.6%, and trivially by the wine share change factor .01%. In essence, this finding suggests that annual changes in per capita total alcohol consumption are unrelated to beverage source. In other words, an ounce of raw alcohol is just that regardless of whether it comes from beer, wine, or liquor. Lastly, the finding suggests that changes in total consumption are driven by forces other than beverage choice.

The regression analysis using change in consumption factor scores is given in Table 4.6. Recall as pointed out in Chapter 3 that factor scores are normalized

Table 4.5
Factor Analysis of Change in Share of Consumption and Total Consumption

		Beer vs Liquor	Wine Share	Total Consumption
Share	Beer	.93	− . 33	− . 17
	Wine	. 00	1. 00	. 00
	Liquor	−. 91	− . 37	. 17
	Total Consumption	− . 19	− . 01	.98
	Variance (%)	49 . 8	31 . 0	19 . 2
	Cum Variance (%)	49 . 8	80 . 8	100 . 0

with zero mean and unit standard deviation. Hence, the standardized and un-standardized coefficients are identical and only one is reported. Further, the intercept terms are always zero and have been omitted from the tables.

The first regression model expresses the relationship between the demand determinant factors and the liquor and total consumption factor, the most important with respect to total consumption since just over half of the variability in total consumption differences was explained by the factor. Only one of the demand factors is related to the consumption factor, namely Trend, which expresses the quadratic or acceleration in the changes in liquor and total consumption. The negative sign of the coefficient suggests that changes in liquor consumption and its associated fraction of total consumption are becoming negative at an increasing rate. In other words, liquor consumption is declining at a faster pace over time and taking a share of total consumption with it. The value of the coefficient, -.649, suggests also that 42.1% of the variability in liquor consumption differences are associated with this accelerating downward trend.

As for advertising, changes in magazine advertising spending are not significantly related to changes in liquor consumption or its associated proportion of total consumption. Although not statistically significant, the relationship is positive and the square of the coefficient for liquor advertising in magazines indicates that about 5.2% of the variability in consumption changes may be accounted for by advertising. Overall, the regression model explained 50.8% of the variability in liquor consumption differences, 38.9% on an adjusted basis, and thus the 5.2% accounted for by advertising represented a tenth of all that was explained by the predictor factors.

The second regression analysis summarized in Table 4.6 involves beer consumption differences and the associated percentage of total consumption changes. Taken as a group, the demand factors explain 43.8% of the variance

Table 4.6
Factor Analytic Regressions for Change in Consumption

		Liquor & Total		Beer & Total		Wine & Total	
		b	t	b	t	b	t
	Beer	-.022	-.17	.029	.21	.075	.49
Ads	Liquor	.227	1.75	.235	1.69	-.239	-1.57
	Wine	-.013	-.10	.138	.99	-.266	-1.75
Population & Liquor Price		-.016	-.12	.556	3.99*	.323	2.13*
Income		.184	1.41	-.056	-.40	.044	.29
Trend		-.649	-4.99*	.171	1.23	-.181	-1.19
Beer Price		.013	.10	-.147	-1.06	.236	1.55
R^2		.508		.438		.328	
Adj R^2		.389		.303		.166	

*$p < .05$

in beer consumption differences and the attributable third of total consumption differences. Individually, only the population and liquor price factor is associated significantly with the beer consumption factor. Generally speaking, larger positive changes in the population of 20- to 34-year-olds are associated with bigger beer consumption differences and, given the negative loading for liquor price on the predictor factor, smaller negative yearly changes in liquor prices relative to the CPI are related to larger beer consumption differences. In short, beer consumption tends to grow with the 20- to 34-year-old segment of the population and decline as liquor becomes inexpensive relative to the CPI.

Beer consumption changes are almost totally unrelated to changes in magazine advertising spending for beer products. Only .08% of the variance in beer consumption differences are related to changes in advertising spending. In fact, beer consumption changes appear to be more closely related to differences in wine and liquor advertising than to advertising for beer products. But of course none of the relationships is statistically significant.

The final regression model reported in Table 4.6 involves wine consumption differences and approximately one-tenth of the total consumption differences accounted for by the yearly changes in wine consumption. Overall, the regression model is the weakest of the three, accounting for only 32.8% of the variance in wine differences and half that, 16.6% when the R^2 statistic is adjusted for the length of the series. As with beer consumption changes, the population and liquor price factor is statistically significant and again positive changes in wine consumption are associated with increases in the 20- to 34-year-old segment of the population and small drops in the relative price of liquor. Population and liquor price changes account for 10.4% of the variability in wine differences.

Like the other two regression models changes in advertising are not significantly related to changes in wine consumption, and indeed two of the relationships are negative, including the coefficient for changes in wine advertising. Thus, positive changes in wine consumption are associated with negative changes in magazine advertising spending for wine products. As always, this relationship, on the surface paradoxical, may be a function of the way advertising was defined or time-dependent relationships in the data, possibilities that will be considered later in the chapter.

Taking stock of the advertising relationships in the three regressions we see that none of the direct relationships, that is, category consumption with category advertising, is statistically significant and moreover only two of three are positive. Further, no cross-category relationship of one beverage type consumption with another's advertising is statistically significant. We can, as a final step in quantifying what little relationship exists, work through the factor loadings and regression coefficients to obtain the amount of variance in total consumption changes that are due to advertising differences. When we multiply the square of the factor loading of total consumption on each factor we obtain the variance in total consumption changes attributable to the factor. This figure can then be multiplied by the square of the regression coefficient for the appropriate advertising factor to obtain the amount of variance in total consumption changes explained by advertising changes.

To illustrate, the factor loading for total consumption differences on the liquor factor is .74 suggesting that 54.8% of the variance ($.74^2$) in changes in total consumption are associated with changes in liquor consumption. From the regression model we also know that the coefficient for the liquor advertising factor is .227 indicating that 5.1% ($.227^2$) of the variability in the liquor consumption factor are due to liquor advertising. Combining the two results we estimate that 2.8% of the variability in total consumption differences is accounted for by changes in liquor advertising ($.548 \times .051$). Using the same methodology for the other two factors we find that beer advertising explains .02% and wine advertising .8% of the variance in total consumption yearly changes, figures that are quite consistent with other researchers (Adlaf and Kohn, 1989; Atkin et al., 1984; Strickland, 1981, 1982).[1]

The regression analyses using factors of demand determinant differences and those for changes in share of consumption and total consumption are shown in Table 4.7. The first factor was responsible for nearly half (49.8%) of the variability in the outcome variables and described a one-for-one share trade-off between beer and liquor consumption. Further, the signs of the factor loadings suggested that beer share (positive loading) had gained at the expense of liquor share (negative loading) over the study period.

When this factor is regressed on the demand factor scores, two relationships are found to be statistically significant. As might be expected, population and liquor price are related to the share trade-off and as has been seen before beer share increases at the expense of liquor share when the population of 20- to 34-year-olds is increased the most and when liquor prices are highest or more correctly drop least. Demographic and liquor price changes account for 13.5% of the variability in beer-liquor share shifts. The second significant variable is Trend indicating that the switch from liquor consumption to beer drinking is accelerating over time, a fact that accounts for 41.0% of the variability in trade-off.

Interestingly, advertising in magazines, either spending or the number of pages, does not appear to influence the share changes in beer and liquor consumption. Again, it would appear that there are limited or negligible advertising impacts at the beverage category level. Taken as a group, the three advertising factors account for only .8% of the variability in the share trade-off factor and this was only 1.4% of the entire variability (58.8%) explained by the model.

The second regression involves the change in wine share factor and in this case advertising seems to play a role. In particular, changes in liquor advertising are related to changes in wine share. The nature of the relationship is such that wine share tends to change positively when liquor advertising changes negatively and this correlation is associated with 10% of the variability in wine share, more than a third of the total 28.4% explained by the entire model. This finding may suggest that while liquor advertising has no direct impact on its own share,

Table 4.7
Factor Analytic Regressions for Change in Share of Consumption and Total Consumption

		Beer (+) vs Liquor (−)		Wine Share		Total Consumption	
		b	t	b	t	b	t
	Beer	.022	.19	.055	.35	.030	.21
Ads	Liquor	−.025	−.21	−.317	−2.02*	.227	1.60
	Wine	.081	.68	−.267	−1.70	−.001	−.01
Population & Liquor Price		.367	3.08*	.176	1.12	.499	3.52*
Income		−.163	−1.37	.020	.13	.088	.62
Trend		.640	5.37*	−.082	−.52	−.325	−2.29*
Beer Price		−.099	−.83	.268	1.71	−.018	−.13
R^2		.588		.284		.416	
Adj R^2		.488		.112		.275	

*p < .05

it plays a protective role against other category intrusion on its portion of total consumption.

The last factor analytic regression considered in Table 4.7 involves changes in total consumption. Results in this instance are quite similar to those for the beer-liquor share trade-off model with one important change in sign for a co-efficient. First, the population and liquor price difference factor is again significant and positive. Total consumption changes most in a positive direction when increases in the 20- to 34-year-old segment of the population are largest and when changes in relative liquor prices decline the most. The population and liquor price change factor accounts for nearly a quarter, 24.9%, of all the variability in total consumption differences. The quadratic trend factor is also statistically significant but unlike the beer-liquor trade-off model the sign of the coefficient is negative indicating that total consumption has declined at an increasing rate, that is, the differences have become negative and larger over the four decades studied.

The change in total consumption factor analytic regression provides probably the best test yet reported on the relationship between advertising and total consumption. If the single distribution theory is correct for advertising to affect alcohol-related adverse outcomes, it must first increase total consumption. The regression model provides no evidence that this is the case. No advertising change factor is significantly related to changes in total consumption. Taken as a group, the variance explained by the advertising factors, after the total consumption factor loading is considered, is 5.0% of total consumption differences and this is almost exclusively due to changes in liquor advertising. A variance explained figure of 5.0% is above that reported in the literature but not excessively so, the range of estimates given in quasi-experimental studies being .2–4.0%

To briefly recap the factor analytic regressions before going on to the supplementary analyses, it would appear that changes in advertising are only weakly associated with changes in consumption. This conclusion pertains to beverage category consumption, total consumption, and share of consumption. The only factor that appears to be consistently associated with changes in consumption or share involves changes in demographics and the relative price of liquor. Generally, larger positive changes in the consumption of beer, wine, total consumption, and share shifts from liquor to beer are associated directly with population shifts and inversely with liquor prices. Thus, consumption increases as does beer share with an increase in the 20- to 34-year-old population segment and the smallest declines in liquor prices.

In no instance was an advertising factor related to consumption, either its own or that of other beverage categories, and its proportionate share of total consumption. In fact, if we calculate the amount of variance in differences of a beverage type consumption explained by changes in advertising for the same type of product, we find 5.1%, .08%, and 7.1% for liquor, beer, and wine, respectively. When these fractions are used to filter the impact on total consumption, we estimate that liquor advertising differences explain 2.8% of the variability in total consumption differences while beer advertising changes explain .02% and wine .8%.

Only one advertising relationship is significant when changes in share of consumption are analyzed. Wine share differences are inversely related to liquor advertising changes. It may be then that the effect of liquor advertising is less to build demand for distilled spirits than to prevent share inroads by other products, namely wine.

Finally, the change in share analysis isolated a pure total consumption factor. Total consumption differences were not significantly related to any advertising factor. On a variance explained basis, roughly 5% of the total consumption differences were associated with changes in the three advertising factors, although the relationship was almost exclusively with liquor advertising differences. Nonetheless, it would appear that over the nearly 40 years studied advertising differences are not associated with changes in total consumption and minimally affect the amount of absolute alcohol consumed per person annually. By implication, if the single distribution theory of alcoholism prevalence is to be believed, advertising might be expected to have a minimal impact on alcohol-related adverse outcomes.

SUPPLEMENTARY ANALYSES

As was done in Chapter 3, we will attempt to corroborate the findings in the primary demand models and factor analytic regressions by examining different specifications of advertising and time-dependent relationships in the first differenced data. The results of the analyses investigating these two issues are given in order in this section.

With respect to alternative ways of defining advertising, Table 4.8 presents the regression analyses for the change in consumption of the three beverage categories with four different specifications of advertising. The first of these, Magazine Ad $, was taken from the primary demand models in Table 4.1. The second, Magazine Pages, was combined with the first in the factor analysis and factor analytic regressions. Total 6 Media and Total Media measure changes in advertising spending in a wide range of media options, including magazines. Total 6 Media and Total Media provide the best estimate of actual spending available for the three beverage categories, therefore, but the study period is constrained to only two decades, 1970–1990.

Regardless of advertising specification or duration of time period there is no statistically significant relationship between changes in advertising and consumption differences for any of the three beverage types. In fact, in only one case, liquor consumption, are the signs of the coefficients the same for the four models. Squaring the standardized regression coefficients for beer consumption changes, we find that changes in advertising account for between .1% and 1.2%

Table 4.8

Regression Coefficients for Different Advertising Specifications with Change in Consumption

	Beer		Wine		Liquor	
	beta	**t**	**beta**	**t**	**beta**	**t**
Magazine Ad $	.113	.75	−.296	−1.52	.145	1.15
Magazine Pages	.031	.21	−.256	−1.35	.089	.71
Total 6 Media	−.038	−.14	.414	1.46	.168	.85
Total Media	.036	.13	.403	1.44	.148	.74

*p < .05

of the variance. Comparable figures for liquor consumption differences are .3 to 2.8%.

The relationship between changes in advertising for wine products and annual wine consumption differences are stronger, ranging from 6.6% to 17.1% of the variance explained. However, it should be noted that no consistent relationship between wine advertising and wine consumption exists; the relationship is negative when magazine advertising over 27 years is examined and positive when a wide range of media over a shorter time are investigated. None of the relationships are statistically significant in any event.

When change in share of consumption is considered (Table 4.9), the results are much the same. No relationship with advertising differences is statistically significant and again only the regression coefficients for the advertising and liquor share have the same sign in all four models. The amount of variance in liquor share changes explained by annual advertising differences is minimal, .02% to 1.1%. The amount of variability in beer share changes accounted for by changes in advertising for beer products is less than .1% when magazine advertising over 38 years is studied but is a good deal higher, 12.8% to 17.3%, when more media are included. The relationships in the wine share models continue to be the strongest, 8.1% to 18.1% of the variance explained but again the signs of the regression coefficients are dependent on the advertising specification, magazine versus 6 or more media, and duration of study, 27 or 21 years. As with changes in consumption, there appears to be little empirical evidence to support the notion that changes in advertising are associated with significant changes in beverage category shares.

The crosscorrelations for the first differences in advertising with differences in consumption and share of total consumption are reported in Tables 4.10 and 4.11, respectively. For consumption differences, no relationship with advertising changes at one or two lags is significant. There is no evidence to suggest therefore that a change in advertising in one year will have an impact on consumption changes a year or two later for any of the three beverage types. For the duration in which advertising has been shown to have an effect, there is no reason to believe that advertising has a temporally prior causal relationship to consumption.

There is, nevertheless, one significant contemporaneous correlation, advertising differences with liquor consumption changes. Annual changes in liquor consumption are positively and significantly correlated with changes in magazine advertising spending in the same year. However, we have already seen in Table 4.1 that this relationship disappears when other factors are controlled in a regression model.

Also in Table 4.10 there are two interesting significant leading crosscorrelations. As seen in Table 3.10, wine consumption changes lead advertising for wine products by one year and liquor consumption changes precede annual differences in advertising for liquor products by two years. Again, it would appear that advertising spending levels, at least in magazines, are set in a budg-

Table 4.9

Regression Coefficents for Different Advertising Specifications with Change in Share of Consumption

	Beer		Wine		Liquor	
	beta	t	beta	t	beta	t
Magazine Ad $	−.026	−.20	−.285	−1.35	.106	.93
Magazine Pages	.015	.11	−.300	−1.49	.015	.13
Total 6 Media	.358	1.24	.426	1.39	.062	.28
Total Media	.416	.17	.411	1.36	.043	.20

*p < .05

Table 4.10
Crosscorrelations of Change in Consumption with Change in Advertising

	Time Difference (Years)	Beer	Wine	Liquor
Lead	2	−.18	.15	.28*
	1	−.07	.36*	.14
	0	.01	−.25	.29*
Lag	−1	−.21	.00	.00
	−2	−.12	−.19	−.03

*p <.05

Table 4.11

Crosscorrelations of Change in Share of Consumption with Change in Advertising

CHANGE IN SHARE

Time Difference (Years)		Beer	Wine	Liquor
Lead	2	–.12	.09	.13
	1	–.10	.24	.02
	0	.03	–.24	.25
Lag	–1	–.17	–.03	.10
	–2	.12	–.15	.06

etary context for wine and liquor products. Marketers seem to be reading past sales results and setting advertising spending targets accordingly. In essence then, consumption of wine and liquor appears to determine advertising for these beverage categories and not vice versa.

The crosscorrelations for change in share of consumption and advertising are reported in Table 4.11. None of the crosscorrelations, leads, lags, or contemporaneous, for any of the three beverage categories is statistically significant. Thus, it would seem that changes in advertising do not influence changes in category consumption nor do share of consumption differences influence annual advertising spending level changes. If advertising is set in a budgetary manner, then it is in reference to sales for individual products and not in terms of share of total consumption.

SUMMARY

In this chapter we investigated the yearly change in advertising and related it to changes in consumption and share of total consumption. Analyzing annual change, or first differences, is a more rigorous definition of the data than that used in the foregoing chapter. The investigation is focused only on that portion of the time series that varies from year to year. The effects of broad social and economic trends tend to be, if not eliminated, at least minimized. As a consequence, statistically significant relationships observed among first differences are more apt to be indicative of "true effects."

It is not surprising then that when the data are transformed by differences many of the significant relationships involving advertising seen in the preceding chapter disappear and the diminishing number of significant results is by no means confined to the advertising variables. The demand models clearly show that consumption and share of consumption are driven by only a small set of social or economic factors which in turn, differ depending on the beverage type.

Looking at the demand models for change in consumption, we see that beer consumption is only related to demographic changes, with alcohol consumption tending to rise with larger numbers of 20- to 34-year-olds. Wine consumption differences are unrelated to changes in any demographic or economic factor. Liquor consumption, as we have seen before, is determined primarily by economic factors, increasing with the growing affluence of the American public and with prices falling relative to the CPI.

It would seem that history favors liquor consumption since the average adult doubled their personal disposable income in real terms from 1950 to 1990 and liquor prices declined sixty percent with respect to the CPI. And yet we also see in the demand models that liquor consumption has changed almost not at all over the period ($b_0 = .001$) and, in fact, liquor consumption has declined at an accelerating rate in later years. Obviously there is more to demand determination than supply (relative prices) and demand (personal disposable income).

Advertising, as measured by changes in real magazine spending, is also unrelated to consumption. In no instance is the relationship between advertising and consumption differences statistically significant. Moreover, advertising changes only explain small amounts of the variance in consumption differences for the three beverage types, 1.3% for beer, 2.1% for liquor, and 8.8% for wine. But even in the case where advertising changes explain the most variation in consumption, for wine, the relationship is negative such that positive changes in advertising are associated with negative changes in wine drinking.

Another way to assess the importance of advertising to consumption is to interpret the unstandardized regression coefficients. For beer a yearly increase of $1 million in real advertising spending would yield an incremental .05 gallons or 6.4 ounces per adult per year in absolute alcohol consumption via beer drinking. The comparable figure for liquor is .02 gallons or 2.6 ounces per year. As always it is important to recall that these are correlations not effects and indeed, when we look at time-ordered relationships the question of advertising causing consumption is doubtful, although the reverse may not be.

The null findings continue when changes in share of total consumption are examined. Again, no magazine advertising spending differences are statistically related to share changes for any of the three types of beverages. The amount of variance explained remains small, .06% for beer, 1.1% for liquor, and 8.1% for wine. The principal impact of advertising has always been assumed to be on share. Our analysis would suggest that if advertising affects share, it is does so at the brand level and not category share of total consumption.

The factor analytic regressions enable us to consider total consumption in the analysis and therefore provide the most direct assessment of the single distribution theory. In the consumption regressions, each beverage type accounted for a fraction of total alcohol consumption, approximately one half (54.8%), a third (34.8%), and a tenth (10.9%) for liquor, beer, and wine drinking, respectively. These mutually independent variables were then regressed on seven equally uncorrelated demand determinant factors, among which were factors representing advertising for the three types of beverages. As usual, no advertising factor was related to its own beverage consumption factor and there were no cross-category effects. Working back through the factor loading and regression coefficients it was possible to determine the liquor advertising factor explained 2.8% of the variability in total consumption, while the beer advertising factor accounted for .03% and wine advertising factor .6%. These estimates are consistent with those reported in the literature.

The second direct test of the single distribution theory is offered by the factor analysis of share of consumption and total consumption. A three factor solution was obtained. The primary factor, accounting for 49.8% of the variability in the original data, described a one-for-one trade-off in beer and liquor shares. Changes in wine share were represented by a second factor that was completely independent of the beer-liquor dynamic. In essence, these two factors suggest that any change in beer share will result in an equal and opposite share change for liquor, while any changes in wine share, in reality quite minor, will be unaffected by and will not affect beer or liquor share.

Last and most importantly, total consumption differences defined a third factor that was similarly unrelated to share shifts, in this case, with changes in share of any of the three beverages. This finding strongly suggests that total alcohol consumption is independent of source or alternately that total consumption would not be impacted if consumers shifted their drinking preferences from one beverage type to another. Total consumption is something of a constant, therefore, which can be satisfied by any of three options.

The regression of the share and total consumption factors on demand determinant factors revealed that demographics and relative liquor prices was the most influential factor, being related to both the beer-liquor trade-off dynamic and total consumption. Wine share was negatively related to liquor advertising, suggesting that if advertising played a role in share changes over time, it was to protect liquor consumption from inroads by wine products. Again, total consumption was not significantly related to any advertising factor and the amount of variance explained by the three advertising variables ranged from 0 to 5.0%.

The strongest relationships observed were for liquor advertising, with a 2.8 to 5.0% range. This may be a function of the advertising specification, which included only magazine advertising spending and pages and the fact that the vast majority, in excess of seven-tenths, of all advertising spending for liquor products is in magazines, whereas only minor proportions of beer and wine spending are in the same medium. Nevertheless, it bears repeating that none of the relationships is significant and the variance explained figures are quite consistent with past research. Extending the implications of the results a step further, if so little of the variance in total consumption is explained by advertising and we can expect a less than perfect correlation between total consumption and mortality, the relationship between advertising and mortality must be attenuated considerably, an issue we will take up in the next chapter.

The last topics considered in this chapter involved different definitions of advertising and the investigation of time dependencies. With respect to the former, recomputing the demand models with magazine pages instead of magazine advertising spending did not alter the substantive findings. No advertising change was related to changes in consumption or share of consumption for the same beverage type. Considering media other than magazines, including six media that were routinely monitored since 1970, all media spending from 1970 to 1990 together corroborate the general conclusion that advertising is unrelated to category consumption or share of consumption.

Time series analysis examining leads and lags revealed some superficially contradictory results, namely that changes in consumption for wine and liquor actually precede changes in advertising for products in the category by one year in the first case and two in the second. This finding might be dismissed as an artifact of the data had it not been reported on several other occasions in the literature. The most reasonable explanation for the significant finding is that advertising spending levels are set as part of an overall budgeting process for marketing expenditures. Past sales are used to forecast those for the current year and anticipated revenue is used as a guideline to set the amount of advertising spending that is affordable. From a time-ordered perspective therefore consumption affects advertising and not the reverse.

Chapter 5

Alcohol-Related Disease Mortality

In this chapter we will consider rates of death from alcohol-related disease and see if we can determine, in even the crudest and most rudimentary way, if advertising for alcohol products is related to these mortality rates. We embark on this investigation with considerable trepidation. Research careers have been spent quite productively examining alcohol-related mortality. As media professionals primarily we do not pretend to be authorities in the field.

All the same, we believe the pursuit is worth the incumbent risks, analytical and professional, since it is critical, we think, to test the entire causal chain in one analytic framework. If nothing else we hope our investigation will encourage others more knowledgeable than ourselves to examine the issue as well. Our approach is exploratory rather than directed and the results are suggestive not definitive. We present both for their heuristic value.

In the following discussion, mortality rates for three alcohol-related diseases will be described first. The source of the data will be given, limitations mentioned, and transformations performed outlined. A descriptive analysis of the data is then given to illustrate numerically and pictorially how mortality has changed over the study period. The second step in the analysis will be to relate mortality rates to alcohol consumption and to this end the results of several time series analyses will be reported. The last section of the chapter provides a simulation of what might happen to annual fatalities and mortality rates if advertising and prices of alcohol products changed. To do this we will use the demand models estimated for raw data to fill out the paths in Figure 1.3 and then forecast potential impact on mortality as effects are filtered through the chain of causality.

We have chosen to investigate three causes of death only, cirrhosis of the liver with alcohol specified, alcoholism or as it later became known alcohol dependence syndrome, and alcoholic psychosis. It was felt that alcohol consumption is directly implicated in these diseases and any consumption or, finally, advertising effect would be seen most readily with these causes of death. If it would ever be possible to detect an advertising effect on mortality it would be for these diseases, therefore.

Alcohol consumption, and by extension advertising, is implicated in many other causes of death as well as monumental economic costs from lost prod'ic-tivity, medical care expenses and premature death. The investigation of these topics is highly complex and unlikely to produce clear results. To illustrate, traffic fatalities would need to consider an alcohol attributable factor (the percentage of fatal accidents involving alcohol). Further, fatalities are highly correlated with highway speed, requiring the control of this variable. Complexities of this sort put the study of all but the most obvious adverse outcomes well beyond the scope of this investigation.

DATA DESCRIPTION

Counts for the three causes of death were obtained from the annual *Vital Statistics of the United States, General Mortality from Selected Causes.* In the classification scheme, cirrhosis of the liver with alcohol specified is identified by codes 571.0 to 571.3 and alcohol psychosis by code 291. Alcoholism was code 322 until 1968 when the code was changed to 303. The disease continued to be called alcoholism until 1979 when the name of code 303 was changed to alcohol dependence syndrome (ADS). The definitional variations created data anomalies that could not be adjusted.[1]

At the time the analysis was performed, mortality statistics were available only through 1989 thereby limiting the study of causes of death to 40 years. Mortality rates were calculated so as to be consistent with other rates used in the analysis, that is, on an adult ($\geq$ 15 years old) per capita basis. All rates are expressed as number of annual deaths per 100,000 adults. Descriptive statistics for mortality counts and rates are presented in Table 5.1 and mortality rates over time are plotted in Figure 5.1.

On average, alcoholic cirrhosis caused 9,332 deaths per year for an annual rate of 6.12 deaths for every 100,000 persons above the age of 14. Alcoholism/ADS killed about a third as many, and alcoholic psychosis one-twentieth. Looking at the former, about 3,500 people per year die of the disease while the adult mortality rate for alcoholism/ADS averaged 2.32 deaths per 100,000. Alcoholic psychosis accounted for 417 deaths every year or a rate of .29 deaths per 100,000 adults. Combined 13,249 deaths per year on average were caused by the three alcohol-related diseases, yielding a total rate per 100,000 adults of 8.73.

Over the four decades studied mortality rates changed markedly, as shown in Figure 5.1, with substantial growth evident for each cause of death. Alcoholic cirrhosis mortality increased steadily from 1950 through 1974, nearly tripling

Table 5.I
Descriptive Statistics for Annual Deaths and Mortality Rates for Alcohol-Related Disease

Annual Deaths	Mean	Standard Deviation	Low	High	Years
Cirrhosis	9,331.75	3,282.81	3,199	13,289	40
ADS/Alcoholism	3,500.37	1,109.29	1,941	5,362	40
Alcoholic Psychosis	417.23	112.42	229	652	40

Annual Morality Rate Per 100,000 Population ≥ 15)					
Cirrhosis	6.12	1.51	2.89	8.32	40
ADS/Alcoholism	2.32	.46	1.67	3.15	40
Alcoholic Psychosis	.29	.09	.18	.45	40

Figure 5.1
Alcohol-Related Mortality Rates

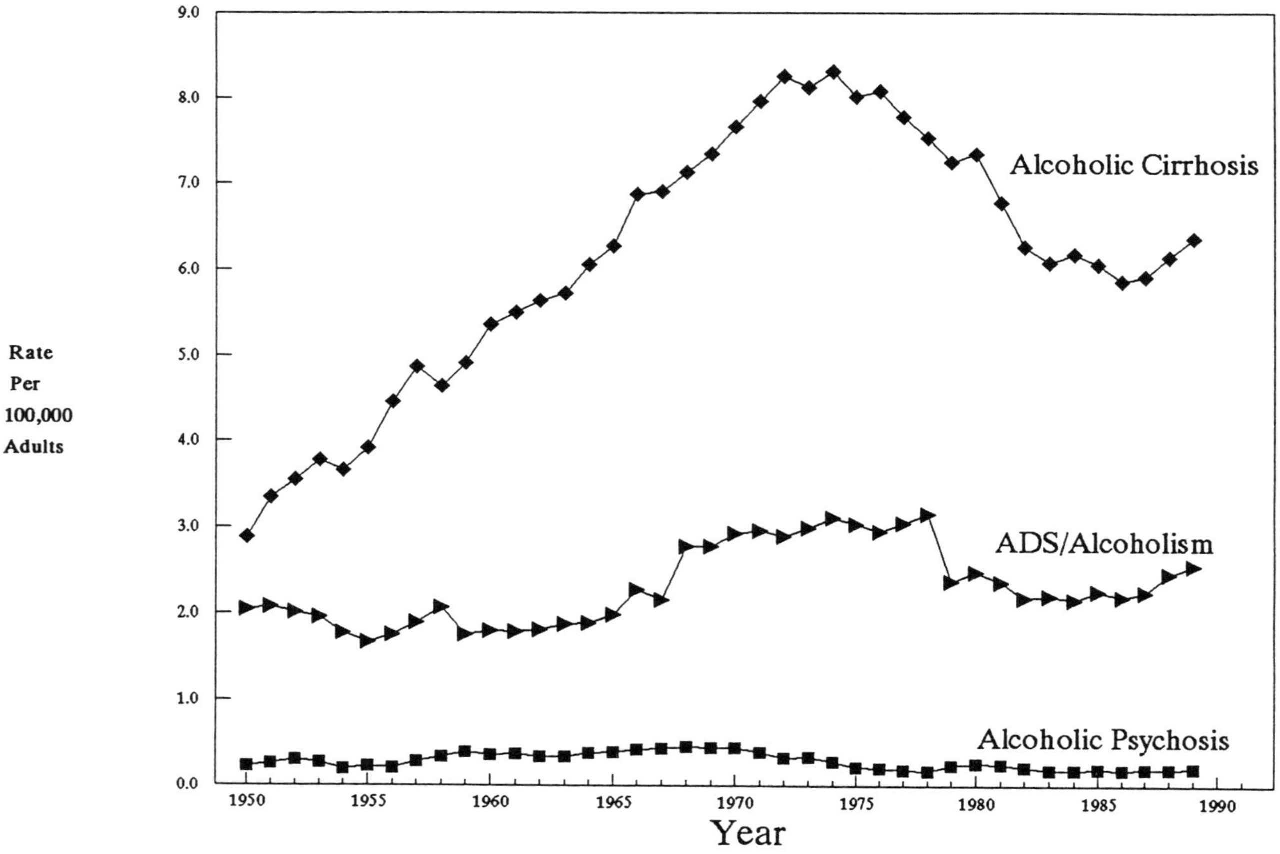

over the period, the rate increasing from 2.89 to 8.32 per 100,000 adults. From 1975 through 1986 the alcoholic cirrhosis rate declined only to begin to rise again for the last three years of the study. Death rates for alcoholism/ADS also grew over the period from a low of 1.67 deaths per 100,000 adults to a high of 3.15. However, the most significant changes in the alcoholism/ADS series accompany the definitional changes in 1967 and 1978. The alcoholic psychosis death rate appears quite flat but its small size disguises a large proportionate change over time. The rate increased two and a half times during the period from a low of .18 deaths per 100,000 adults to a high of .45.

It is interesting to compare the mortality rates, especially alcoholic cirrhosis, with the annual per capita consumption figures shown in Figure 2.7. Both seem to have the same general form increasing and subsequently declining over time. However, the total consumption series appears to follow alcoholic cirrhosis mortality. Cirrhosis mortality increases from 1950 until 1974, whereas per capita consumption of total alcohol does not begin to rise until 1961. What is more, per capita consumption does not reach its peak until 1981, at which point alcoholic cirrhosis rates were in the sixth year of a downward cycle. Alcohol consumption, finally, appeared to reach bottom in 1989, three years after alcoholic cirrhosis rates. Obviously there is no strong visual evidence that consumption leads and therefore causes mortality from alcohol-related disease, and as we will see next, time series methods do little to resolve the mystery.

CONSUMPTION AND MORTALITY

In order to investigate time dependencies in the data set, total alcohol consumption was crosscorrelated with mortality rates for the three alcohol-related causes of death. The results of the crosscorrelations for raw data[2] and first differences are given in Table 5.2. For this analysis, only crosscorrelations in which consumption preceded mortality were considered, since the converse is incomprehensible. Stated somewhat differently, we could not envision a plausible explanation of why mortality from alcohol-related disease would temporally precede aggregate consumption of the agent causing death.

The lagged correlations given in Table 5.2 provide little evidence, either for raw data or first differences, that total alcohol consumption is temporally prior to and significantly related to alcohol-related mortality rates. For cirrhosis we find only one significant correlation, for both raw data and first differences, at lag one year, but in both cases the correlation is negative, suggesting increased mortality rates are associated with decreased total alcohol consumption the year before and vice versa. Only one correlation is significant for alcoholism/ADS, raw data at lag nine years, and again the coefficient is negative. Lastly, the only significant crosscorrelation involving total mortality with alcoholic psychosis is contemporaneous for raw data.

An investigation of lagged effects at the category level, summarized in Table 5.3, is not much more revealing. There are a smattering of significant correla-

Table 5.2
Crosscorrelations of Total Alcohol Consumption and Alcohol-Related Mortality

Time Difference	RAW DATA			FIRST DIFFERENCES		
	Cirrhosis	Alcoholism/ADS	Alcoholic Psychosis	Cirrhosis	Alcoholism/ADS	Alcoholic Psychosis
0	.14	−.12	.32*	.19	−.06	.21
−1	−.37*	.00	.09	−.36*	.00	.07
−2	.18	.14	.00	.23	.15	−.02
−3	.13	.13	−.03	.15	.14	−.01
−4	.21	−.15	−.13	.24	−.09	−.10
−5	−.10	.07	.19	−.03	.08	.19
−6	−.15	.10	−.10	−.08	.14	−.07
−7	.14	−.04	.17	.24	−.03	.19
−8	.18	.11	−.22	.21	.14	−.19
−9	.03	−.31*	−.08	.11	−.21	−.10
−10	.00	.27	−.02	−.01	.22	−.01
−11	−.17	−.21	.16	−.10	−.12	.14
−12	.03	.10	.17	.02	.01	.22

* $p < .05$

Table 5.3
Crosscorrelations of Category Alcohol Consumption and Mortality Rates

	Alcoholic Cirrhosis		Alcoholism/ ADS		Alcoholic Psychosis	
	td	r	td	r	td	r
Raw Data						
Beer	−5	−.29	−9	−.30	0	.35
					−11	.32
Wine	−	−	−	−	−	−
Liquor	−1	−.37	−	−	−	−
First Differences						
Beer	−1	−.33	−6	.36	−11	.29
	−3	.31				
	−7	.30				
Wine	−	−	−10	.32	−.12	.30
Liquor	0	.28	−	−	−	−
	−1	−.30				
	−4	.29				

tions but given the number that were computed this is hardly surprising. Also puzzling is that 5 of the 15 significant correlations are negative, three of which are for alcoholic cirrhosis at lag one year. If there is any semblance of a time dependency it would appear to be for alcoholism/ADS and alcoholic psychosis in the 9- to 12-year lag range. Combined with the results for total consumption, it does not appear that there are strong time-dependent relationships and certainly not ones that need to be taken into account in the analysis.

We are at a loss to explain these findings. Perhaps the effects of consumption are cumulative and not observable as discrete lags. Possibly too the effect of consumption on mortality is manifest only among a predisposed segment of the population whose health is deteriorated from long-term abuse of alcohol and therefore not distinct when rates for the general population are studied. A similar argument holds for mortality rates within age bands. It may be as well that our time series is simply not long enough to allow the lag structure time to be revealed.[3]

To examine the last possibility in greater detail we obtained age-adjusted mortality rates for alcoholic cirrhosis for the period 1934–1990 (Savage et al., 1993). Per capita consumption figures were available for the same length of time

(Williams et al., 1993). The two time series are plotted against each other in Figure 5.2, the last portion of which from 1950 onward parallels the data presented in Figures 2.7 and 5.1.

As we inspect the two lines it is clear they follow generally similar paths. Note, however, by superimposing the two series the consumption lags mortality phenomenon after 1950 is clearly evident especially from 1970 onward. Before 1950 consumption exhibits three distinct peaks. In one instance, consumption leads mortality by two years, 1945–1947. The others appear to be contemporaneous, 1947 and 1936–1937.

In fact, there is a deep structure between the age-adjusted cirrhosis mortality series and total consumption. When the data were exponentially smoothed and a Box-Jenkins model fit to the residuals significant correlations were observed at 1-, 2-, 6-, and 11-year lags and the 6-year lag was very strong, .564. However, when the same technique was applied to the data used in this study, no structure was found for alcoholism/ADS and alcoholic psychosis and a contemporaneous effect was evident for alcoholic cirrhosis.

So once again our efforts to find any meaningful temporally prior causality between total consumption and mortality from alcohol-related disease is frustrated. We chose to proceed with the analysis, consequently, by examining only contemporaneous effects, that is, without the benefits of lagged effects for consumption. This decision assumes total alcohol consumption has no measurable cumulative effect on mortality. In essence, a death is presumed to be caused by the consumption of alcohol in a given year and if mortality is related to long-term use it is as a function of current drinking killing individuals whose health has been damaged by chronic alcohol use.

SIMULATION

The last stage in our investigation is to link the various discrete stages of the investigation and subsequently attempt to estimate the likely consequences of changes in demand predictors. In essence, the causal model given in Figure 1.3 is filled out with the contingent probabilities of moving from one step to the next or along a particular path obtained from the demand models and analysis of total consumption and mortality (Figure 5.3). To do this, we first take the individual demand models and estimate category consumption under some predetermined set of conditions. Next, category consumption is used to predict total consumption which, in turn, is related to mortality for each of the three causes of death. Finally, the preconditions are manipulated to forecast how mortality might be affected if advertising were to change.

For the purposes of the simulation, we will concentrate on measuring the impact of changes in two variables exclusively. The variables selected for manipulation, price and advertising, are the demand determinants most easily altered by policy. It would be possible then for a governmental body to regulate price, for example, by raising taxes on alcohol products, or limit exposure to

Figure 5.2
Age-Adjusted Alcoholic Cirrhosis Mortality Rate and Total per Capita Alcohol Consumption

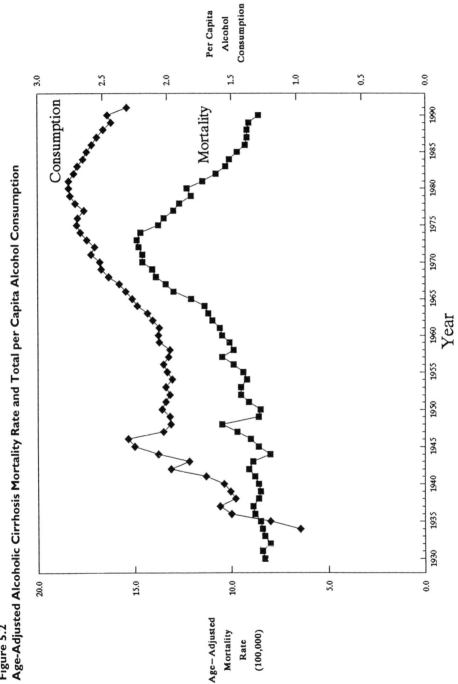

Figure 5.3
Transitional Probabilities (R²) for Conceptual Model Paths

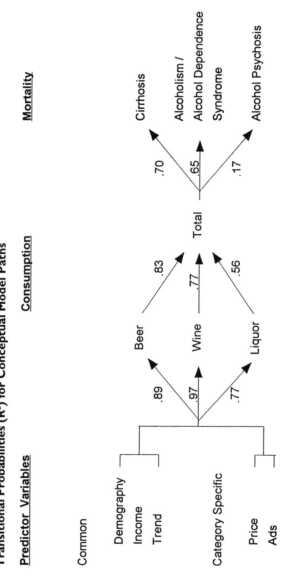

alcohol messages, say, by banning broadcast advertising. In contrast, any action taken to effect affluence, such as, by raising taxes generally, would be less immediate and specific, while demographic trends are largely beyond the scope of governmental purview. Constructing the analysis in this fashion gives us an opportunity as a result to evaluate the efficacy of consumption control policy options.

During the simulation then Income and Population were treated as constants and Price and Magazine Ad $ were manipulated. In particular, Income and Population were held at their historical mean values for the study period. The first forecast run established a base case and in this model Price and Magazine Ad $ were held at their historical averages as well. The historical averages used as control values for the demand determinants are given in Table 5.4.

After the base case was calculated eight scenarios were tested: for Price, what would happen if each category alone experienced a 10% drop in prices relative to the CPI and then if all three beverage types experienced a 10% price decline simultaneously; for Magazine Ad $, what would happen if ad spending for a beverage category alone increased by 10% and then if advertising in magazines for all three categories increased 10% at the same time. When either Price or Magazine Ad $ was manipulated the other variable was held constant at its historical mean. The last stage in the simulation was to measure the impact of the price or advertising change, which was accomplished by calculating the difference between the forecasted deaths and mortality rate with those obtained for the base case.

Table 5.5 summarizes the results of the simulation, base case and scenarios. On average over the period when all demand predictors are held constant at their historical means we project that 9,495 people would die annually of alcoholic cirrhosis and that this figure would translate into a rate of 6.221 deaths per 100,000 adults. Figures for the other two causes of death computed under the same base case scenario are 3,558 deaths per annum for alcoholism/ADS and 429 for alcoholic psychosis or, rates per 100,000 adults of 2.331 and .281, respectively. The combined mortality of the three diseases is 13,482 or a rate of 8.833 fatalities per 100,000 adults under historically average conditions.

Now suppose magazine advertising increased by 10% for one product category only. For wine this would mean that real advertising spending would increase $2.17 million from $21.7 million to $23.87 million. When this change is effected and other factors including price and advertising for the other two product categories are held constant, we predict there would be 9,503 deaths per year from alcoholic cirrhosis for a rate of 6.355 per 100,000 adults. If advertising increased by 10% for all product categories real spending in magazines would increase by $20.81 million, jumping from a baseline of $208.1 million to $228.91 million. Under these conditions we forecast there would be 9,705 deaths from alcoholic cirrhosis per year for a rate of 6.358.

Looking now at price effects, if beer price were to drop 10% from its histor-

Table 5.4
Historical Average Values for Demand Determinants

	Average
Year	1972
Population (000,000)	
20–34	46.721
>15	152.629
Income (1982 Dollars)	$12,439.00
PRICE (/CPI)	
Beer	1.23
Wine	1.22
Liquor	1.61
MAGAZINE AD $ (000,000 1982 Dollars)	
Beer	13.9
Wine	21.7
Liquor	172.5

ical average, the ratio relative to the CPI would fall from 1.23 to 1.107. That is, prices would decline from 23% above the CPI for all consumer products to just 10.7% above. If this were to occur for beer prices alone we project the annual deaths from alcoholic cirrhosis would rise to 10,506 per year for a rate of 6.883. If prices for all three beverage classes were to decline 10% at the same time alcoholic cirrhosis deaths would jump to 11,882 or a rate of 7.784 deaths per 100,000 adults. The remaining entries in Table 5.5 are computed in the same manner, blank entries are given when the model, due to negative coefficients, actually predicted fewer deaths than occurred in fact.

It is clear from Table 5.5 that advertising effects are not terribly large and pale in comparison to the predicted impact of price reductions. To clarify this issue incremental values for death and mortality rates for each scenario over and above the base case are given in Table 5.6. Also given in the table is the percentage in incremental mortality forecast under each condition as well as summary columns showing the impact on the three alcohol-related causes of death combined.

Using alcoholic cirrhosis and liquor as an example, we can see that a 10% increase in advertising could result in an additional 206 deaths per year, the mortality rate might increase by .134 deaths per 100,000 adults and these increases would be 2.1% above the base case deaths and mortality rate. Note also that virtually the entire change in mortality due to advertising is accounted for

Table 5.5
Annual Deaths and Mortality Rates for Base Case and Scenarios

	Alcoholic Cirrhosis		Alcoholism/ ADS		Alcoholic Psychosis	
	Deaths	Rate	Deaths	Rate	Deaths	Rate
Base	9,495	6.221	3,558	2.331	429	.281
10% Increase in Advertising						
Beer Only	–	–	3,558	2.331	429	.281
Wine Only	9,503	6.226	3,561	2.333	429	.281
Liquor Only	9,701	6.355	3,632	2.380	433	.284
All Three	9,705	6.358	3,632	2.380	433	.284
10% Reduction in Price						
Beer Only	10,506	6.883	3,921	2.569	446	.292
Wine Only	–	–	–	–	–	–
Liquor Only	11,002	7.208	4,100	2.686	454	.297
All Three	11,882	7.784	4,958	2.893	468	.307

Table 5.6
Predicted Change in Mortality from Base Case with Advertising and Price Changes

	Alcoholic Cirrhosis			Alcoholism/ ADS			Alcoholic Psychosis			Total		
	Deaths	Rate	%	Deaths	Rate	%	Deaths	Rate	%	Deaths	Rate	%
10% Increase in Advertising												
Beer Only	—	—	—	—	—	—	—	—	—	—	—	—
Wine Only	8	.005	.1	3	.002	.1	—	—	—	11	.007	.1
Liquor Only	206	.134	2.1	74	.049	2.1	4	.003	.7	284	.186	2.1
All Three	210	.137	2.2	74	.049	2.1	4	.003	.9	288	.189	2.1
10% Reduction in Price												
Beer Only	1,011	.662	10.6	363	.238	10.2	17	.011	3.8	1,391	.911	10.3
Wine Only	—	—	—	—	—	—	—	—	—	—	—	—
Liquor Only	1,507	.987	15.9	542	.355	15.2	25	.016	5.6	2,074	1.358	15.4
All Three	2,387	1.563	25.1	1,400	.562	24.1	39	.026	9.3	3,826	2.151	24.4

by the predicted change if liquor advertising alone varied. In the case of alcoholic cirrhosis, if advertising spending for all three beverage types were to increase by 10% at the same time we could see an additional 210 deaths a year, just four more than would be forecast if liquor advertising alone increased by 10%.

By comparison, if liquor prices were to drop by 10% relative to the CPI we forecast an additional 1,507 people would die from alcoholic cirrhosis each year. The mortality rate would climb nearly one death per 100,000 adults, .987, or 15.9% above the base level. For liquor then price changes are almost eight times more impactful on mortality rates than are similar proportionate changes in advertising. Further, the effect of price changes would not be confined to liquor products only. Mortality might be expected to increase by 10.6% if beer prices declined by 10% in isolation. Consequently, if all three beverages were to decline in price by 10% relative to the CPI, deaths from alcoholic cirrhosis might jump by 25.1% of which four-tenths would be due to decreases in beer prices and six-tenths to liquor price declines.

It is possible to assess the remaining category contributions to mortality from the three causes of death when advertising and prices change in a like manner. Changes in beer advertising, for instance, are predicted to have no impact on mortality, while changes in beer prices could increase alcoholic cirrhosis and alcoholism/ADS by roughly 10% and alcoholic psychosis deaths by about 4%. A 10% increase in magazine advertising spending for wine is expected to have virtually no effect on mortality for any of the three diseases, .1% increase at most, and none at all if price dropped by 10%. Wine consumption, in short, is not affected by advertising and is inelastic to price changes. Liquor advertising spending could increase alcoholic cirrhosis and alcoholism/ADS by 2.1% and alcoholic psychosis by .7% if it were to rise by 10%. Similar proportionate declines in prices would have approximately 12 times the effect, increasing alcoholic cirrhosis and alcoholism/ADS by about 15% and alcoholic psychosis by just under 6%.

Perhaps the most revealing comparisons available in Table 5.6 are provided in the total rows and columns. We can see that if real advertising spending in magazines increased 10% for all beverage categories simultaneously mortality rates would potentially increase by .9 to 2.1% depending on the disease and 2.1% for all three causes of death combined. To quantify the relationship further if advertising spending in magazines were to increase by $20.8 million in real terms, we might expect an additional 288 people to die from one of the three alcohol-related causes of death. The resulting increase in the combined mortality rate would be .189 per 100,000 adults.

It is worth noting the similarity in this finding to studies of advertising elasticities in the United Kingdom in which a rough 10:1 relationship was found between advertising and consumption increases, such that if advertising increased by 10% consumption would rise by 1%. Of course, the U.K. results are category specific and were seen to lessen across the system of beverage consumption options. The results, in percentage terms, parallel those seen between advertising and adverse outcomes in quasi-experimental studies too. For instance, .2 to 1.2% in the variability of intoxication was shown to be accounted for by advertising and between .1 and 1.2% of the variance other negative outcomes such as drinking and driving (Fisher, 1993). Our results seem to fit comfortably in this context of past findings.

Now suppose prices for all three product categories were to decline 10%, for example, by 12 to 16% of the CPI for all consumer products. We forecast that both alcoholic cirrhosis and alcoholism/ADS would increase by roughly 25% while alcoholic psychosis deaths would increase by just over 9%. And as noted earlier, about four-tenths of the increases in mortality would be due to beer price declines and six-tenths to liquor. Overall we would expect incremental mortality from the three causes combined to be 3,826 deaths or 2.151 additional deaths for every 100,000 adults in the population. Finally, the increase in mortality due to 10% price declines, 24.4%, is 12 times the expected increase of 2.1% if advertising rose 10% for all product categories.

In the end, the simulation model appears to support a series of conclusions regarding advertising and price effects. With regard to the former, a 10% increase in category advertising increases mortality by 0 to 2.1% depending on the disease and category. Second, the vast majority of impact from advertising results from changes in liquor advertising. Increasing beer advertising in magazines does not appear to affect mortality. A 10% increase in advertising for all beverage types could increase deaths by .9 to 2.2% depending on the disease and 2.1% for the three causes of death combined.

Reductions in prices of the same percentage magnitude increase mortality by 3.8 to 15.9% depending on the category affected and the cause of death. Wine price changes do not appear to affect mortality while the incremental impact of liquor is half again as large as that for beer, 5.6 to 15.9% versus 3.8 to 10.6%, depending on the cause of death. Price reductions of 10% for the three beverage types combined could increase mortality by 9.3 to 25.1% depending on the cause and are forecast to raise mortality by 24.4% when the three causes of death are considered together. Price reductions appear to have 12 times the impact on mortality as similar percentage changes in advertising.

SUMMARY

Our goal in this chapter was to provide a complete test of the conceptual model given in Figure 1.3. To this end we linked demand determinants to category consumption, predicted total consumption from the category components, and finally, related total consumption to mortality from alcohol-related disease. The ultimate objective was to determine if advertising could be shown to affect mortality after its impact had traversed the full chain of causality and been modulated by the contingent probabilities of moving from one stage to the next.

We did this with the full awareness that the nature of the relationship between consumption and mortality, to say nothing of advertising, is complex and might appear to be oversimplified by our data and analysis. The results might seem more definitive than we believe them to be. Nevertheless, we feel it essential that the full progression of effects, so often assumed in the literature, be tested in one analytic framework. In the end, the investigation is exploratory in character and the results offered for their heuristic value.

Mortality from three alcohol-related causes of death were examined, specifically cirrhosis of the liver with alcohol specified, alcoholism or equivalently alcohol dependence syndrome (ADS), and alcoholic psychosis. It was felt that the role of consumption, and by extension advertising, would be most easily observed and quantified for these causes of death, particularly when compared with other forms of mortality such as traffic accidents or esophageal cancer in which alcohol consumption is only implicated. If an advertising effect is not apparent for the three causes of death chosen therefore it is unlikely to be measurable for any other type of mortality.

The first step in the analytic phase of the morality study was to relate consumption to mortality. In this regard, it was interesting to note that mortality, especially cirrhosis mortality, tended to rise sharply for the first 20 years of the study. It grew from a rate of just under 3 deaths per 100,000 adults in 1950 to a little over 8 in 1970. Cirrhosis deaths declined for the next 15 years, reaching a rate of 6 per 100,000 by 1986. The cirrhosis mortality rate increased again for each of the last three years of the study. Alcoholism/ADS rates also climbed but more as a function of definitional changes in the cause of death than as a result of a discernible trend. Alcoholic psychosis seemed to follow the pattern of cirrhosis, albeit at a much diminished level.

The next step in the analysis was to measure the association between total alcohol consumption and rates of death from alcohol-related disease and indeed the trend in annual per capita alcohol consumption bears a surface similarity to the variability in mortality rates, especially that of alcoholic cirrhosis. However, visual inspection of the two time series indicated that mortality actually preceded increases in total alcohol consumption in many instances.

This belief was borne out when more complicated time series methods were applied to the data. We could find no large or consistent lagged relationship between total or category consumption and any of the three alcohol-related causes of death. Next we examined a longer time series of age-adjusted alcoholic cirrhosis mortality rate. After exponential smoothing and modeling with Box-Jenkins time series techniques, a strong temporally antecedent relationship was found between per capita consumption and the cirrhosis mortality rate. But application of the same analytic approach to the three shorter cause of death series again revealed no strong structure.

Frustrated by our attempts to model the relationship between per capita consumption and mortality rates in a general time series context, we decided to proceed with the analysis using only contemporaneous effects. We assume as a consequence that total alcohol consumption in any given year is related to death from alcoholic disease in that year only. We may believe otherwise but our data dictate this course.

Using raw contemporaneous data we filled out the contingent probabilities for the paths given in the conceptual model, Figure 1.3. We then ran a series of forecasts to determine what would be the likely impact on mortality rates if advertising increased or price decreased by a specified amount. Price and advertising were chosen for manipulation since they are the demand determinants most easily altered by governmental action. Raising taxes or banning advertising could be expected to have an immediate and direct impact on consumption. In effect, the forecasts enable us to compare the most efficacious means of managing alcohol consumption, if that is truly the objective of legislation.

In all, nine simulations were run: a base case scenario in which the average values for the demand determinants were related to mortality rates, three models in which advertising for one beverage category only was increased 10%, one model in which advertising for all beverage classes was increased 10%, three models in which prices for one beverage category only were assumed to decline by 10%, and a final model in which prices for all these categories of consumption were assumed to decrease by 10% simultaneously. The effect of advertising or price was determined by measuring the difference between base case mortality and mortality after a predictor variable was changed.

The results of the simulation modeling are very revealing and support a number of conclusions. With respect to advertising: a 10% increase for all product categories simultaneously is projected to increase mortality for the three causes of death combined by 2.1%, resulting in 288 more deaths per year and an increase in the combined mortality rate by .189 deaths per 100,000 adults. The impact on the causes of death individually ranged from a low of .9% for alcoholic psychosis to a high of 2.2% for cirrhosis. At the category level, virtually all of the advertising effect is due to the change in liquor advertising. Beer advertising had no effect on mortality and the wine effect was negligible. As always, this finding may be a by-product of how advertising was specified, as spending in magazines, and the disproportionate utilization of the medium as an advertising venue for the three product groups.

It bears repeating, the effect of advertising produced by the simulation, expressed in percentage terms, is quite consistent with past econometric research, which demonstrated a rough 10:1 relationship between advertising and consumption, that is, a 10% increase in advertising yields a 1% increase in consumption. More directly comparable, quasi-experimental studies have shown between .2 to 1.2% of the variance in negative drinking outcomes is associated with advertising exposure. Our results appear to fit well in this diverse yet congruent empirical context.

The impact of price on mortality was much more significant. In fact, the simulation forecasts suggest a 10% decrease in prices of the three beverage categories would have 12 times the impact on mortality of an equal proportional change in advertising. We forecast that mortality could increase by 24.4% overall and as many as 3,826 additional deaths a year or 2.151 deaths per 100,000 adults could result. The biggest impact would be as before on alcoholic cirrhosis and alcoholism/ADS, which are projected to increase 24 to 25%, and less on alcoholic psychosis, which could increase about 9%.

As for individual category effects, about four-tenths of the combined price reduction impact could be due to beer. So a 10% reduction in beer prices might increase mortality from the three causes of death by a like amount, 10.3%. The remaining effect is due to liquor for which a 10% decrease in price might produce a 15% rise in mortality. Changes in wine price appear to have no impact on mortality in our analysis.

Chapter 6

Summary and Conclusions

In this chapter we will review the substantive findings of the investigation and attempt to come to some closure regarding the degree to which advertising affects alcohol consumption and mortality from alcohol-related disease. The analysis is, of course, fixed in place and time and deals with alcohol consumption and mortality in the United States from 1950–1990. With this in mind, we will endeavor to enhance the generalizability of the findings by noting their compatibility with a multidisciplinary body of research on advertising, alcohol consumption and abuse.

The summary begins with a brief reprise of the conceptual model that provides the structure and organizing framework of the study and a schema which, we would suggest, informs much of the research on advertising and alcohol use. The major societal trends, social and economic, that appear to have driven alcohol demand over time are reviewed then along with the trends in alcohol consumption. The next three sections of the chapter draw together the findings regarding alcohol consumption; in order they are category consumption, category share of total consumption, and lastly, total consumption. Mortality is considered next, how it has varied over time, its relationship to consumption, and how it might be expected to change as a result of advertising and price fluctuations. To conclude we will evaluate the null hypothesis posed at the outset of the investigation to determine if it should be accepted or rejected based on the cumulative findings of the study.

CONCEPTUAL MODEL AND STUDY DESIGN

At the high level of aggregation at which the investigation was conducted, the presumed way advertising affects alcohol use and eventually negative outcomes of excessive drinking is quite simple. Exposure to alcohol images in the media, especially persuasive appeals conveyed in ads, are expected to initiate, stimulate, or perpetuate drinking. Over time incremental alcohol consumption will be expressed as increased rates of alcohol-related economic, social, or health problems. In its basic form, the model proposes exposure leads to behavioral acquisition to negative outcomes associated with excessive use.

In the literature two theories have been enlisted to provide the linkage between the points on the conceptual continuum. Social learning theory explains how exposure to alcohol messages is internalized by the viewer and then expressed as drinking behavior. The causal mechanism proposed is operant conditioning and the theory suggests that behavior is acquired and shaped by the consequences that follow it, differential reinforcement. The theory further suggests that complex behavior is learned in interaction with significant others such as peers and parents, who provide a normative context for the behavior as well as models for it.

With respect to media effects, the notion of models takes a more general form. Specifically, behavior can be acquired when a person watches someone perform the behavior, including filmed models or cartoon characters, and observes the consequences that befall the actor. Behavior is thought to be acquired by the viewer or is more likely if the reinforcement received by the filmed model is positive or neutral (non-negative) and is less likely if the consequences experienced by the model are negative.

The media, of course, is presumed to provide a plethora of models to imitate and content analyses do indeed indicate that alcohol images are omnipresent in the contemporary media environment. More importantly, the messages are interpreted as showing alcohol users either being rewarded for their behavior or at least avoiding negative consequences from it. This situation is exacerbated for commercials supposedly. Because manufacturers have an interest in promoting the use of their products, advertising is construed to be a one-sided appeal that makes drinking attractive (e.g., by using celebrity endorsers), implies product benefits that are not consistent with product use (e.g., athletic prowess which in fact is diminished with increased use), or rewards the user.

The cumulative weight of the number of images and their content should make drinking more likely, therefore, according to social learning theory. In this regard, it is important to note that all tests of social learning theory tenets in relation to alcohol consumption have found that imitation or equivalently the acquisition of behavior after watching filmed models is not significantly related to consumption. What is more, the small media effects that have been observed are dwarfed by the contribution of differential reinforcement and differential association to the process.

The framework proposed in the literature to connect behavior with adverse outcomes is the single distribution theory. Per capita alcohol consumption is assumed to be distributed lognormally, while the incidence and prevalence of alcohol abuse is assumed to be a function of average consumption and the percentage of persons in the tail of the distribution whose excessive use is above a threshold that will eventually cause health damage. According to the theory any environmental factor, of which advertising could be one, that raises the mean level of consumption and shifts more individuals beyond the threshold will increase alcohol-related disease.

For our purposes, the single distribution theory has major implications in how the study is designed and the level of aggregation at which it is conducted. The theory posits that total alcohol consumption must increase to cause adverse outcomes. It is not sufficient therefore to demonstrate advertising increases the consumption of a brand, or for that matter even a category of alcohol products. Total consumption summed across the three major beverage groups, beer, wine, and liquor, must increase. For advertising to be implicated in adverse outcomes then it must be shown to raise alcohol consumption in the aggregate.

The single distribution theory also leads us away from the analysis of individual behavior since only average alcohol consumption in a population needs to rise to cause increases in negative outcomes if the theory is correct. It is somewhat irrelevant then precisely how advertising works. It could cause more people to start drinking, promote greater consumption at each occasion, or reinforce drinking so repeat drinking is more likely or the time between occasions decreases. Whatever the effect on the individual level, the summated impact must be to raise total consumption.

Regarding this arm of the conceptual model, research reported in the literature documents a weak relationship between advertising and alcohol consumption and an even more tenuous one between consumption and negative outcomes. Exposure to advertising has been shown to account for .2 to 4.0% of the variability in consumption, .2 to 1.2% of the variance in the frequency of intoxication, and .1 to 1.2% of the variability in other indicators of alcohol abuse.

Results from a second research tradition, the econometric estimation of demand, suggest that advertising influences consumption in a 10:1 ratio, a 10% increase in advertising for a category of products equating to a 1% rise in consumption. Further, since most beverage types are substitutes, the impact of advertising at a category level tends to dampen across the full system of beverage options such that the final effect on total alcohol consumption is minimal. Finally, evaluations of changes in permissible advertising have been unable to document any subsequent change in alcohol consumption. Taken as a whole these results do not support the notion that advertising significantly affects total alcohol consumption or, by extension of the single distribution theory, increases negative outcomes.

If there is a single pervasive shortcoming in the collective research done on the topic it is that the causal chain given in the conceptual model is rarely tested in its entirety. The opportunity lost is most apparent for the econometric tradition, we feel, since its methods are best suited to the measurement of aggregate effects over time required by theory. Our research approach was, as a consequence, to test the full chain of effects shown in Figure 1.3 within an econometric framework.

The analytic operationalization of the conceptual model suggests that alcohol consumption is a function of three determinants that are common to all beverage categories—demography, personal income (demand), and a time trend—and two that are specific to each category—advertising and prices (supply). For each category of consumption we constructed a regression model to determine how the various predictors affected consumption of a particular beverage type. Subsequently we related category consumption to total consumption and finally to mortality from three alcohol-related diseases, cirrhosis of the liver with alcohol specified, alcoholism or alternatively alcohol dependence syndrome, and alcoholic psychosis. Advertising effects were calculated at each stage by working through its effect diminished by the transitional probabilities of moving from one step to the next, Figure 5.3.

SOCIETAL AND CONSUMPTION TRENDS

The regression models built for category consumption in many respects quantify major social and economic trends that occurred in the United States over the four decades studied. Each of the trends was significant in its own right and could have affected consumption. Working in concert the societal dynamics provided a strong impetus toward increased alcohol consumption.

Demographic shifts were apparent as the age composition of the population changed radically. The young adult segment, aged 20 to 34, nearly doubled in size as the post–World War II baby boomers reach the age of majority. Young adults are traditionally the heaviest consumers of alcohol and exhibit distinct preferences for beer products and to a lesser degree wine in favor of distilled alternatives. We might expect per capita consumption to rise accordingly and the structure of the beverage industry to change as share shifted between product categories.

At the same time, the American public enjoyed an almost uninterrupted rise in affluence. Personal disposable income doubled in real terms over the study period, growing from roughly $8,000 per adult in 1950 to about $16,000 in 1990. The impact of growing affluence is again twofold, as a stimulant to consumption and as a category share change agent. In particular, many econometric studies have shown that the proportion of a household's disposable income that is spent on alcohol products remains in a fairly constant range of 6 to 8%. If this figure accurately reflects the historical situation in the United States, it suggests that the average American would have twice as much to spend on alcohol products, in real terms, without increasing the proportionate amount of expenditure. Second, we might expect products that are expensive, liquor, relative to the alternatives, beer and wine, would benefit from the growing affluence.

The economic engine for increased consumption was fueled additionally by falling prices. Over the course of the study, liquor product prices fell 60% as compared with the CPI for all consumer products, while beer and wine prices fell by 40%. Alcoholic beverages generally and liquor specifically became much more attractive on a cost basis when compared with nonalcoholic alternatives. As with affluence, we would expect total consumption to be promoted by this trend and for liquor products to be the primary beneficiary of any movement in consumption.

The last important trend involves the explosive growth of media and advertising since 1950. This growth can be characterized in two ways: a dramatic increase in the number of venues available to convey advertising and in an increased willingness of manufacturers to spend corporate resources to persuade consumers. Considering the former, advertising in only one medium could be tracked for the entire study period, but by 1990 there were ten individual media with sufficiently large advertising expenditures to warrant continuous monitoring. Meanwhile in just the last 20 years manufacturers' advertising spending tripled from $446.4 million to $1,225.7 million, the vast majority of this increase being attributable to increased spending for beer products. To the degree advertising affects consumption we might expect an increase in total consumption and a shift in share to beer products as a result.

The four major trends represent something of a mutually reinforcing spur to greater consumption, therefore, as well as being agents of change in industry structure. The hypothesized impact of each trend on consumption and share of consumption is summarized in Table 6.1. To characterize the joint impact on consumption: an increase in the heaviest consuming segment of the population coincided with an increasingly affordable product due to growing consumer affluence and a steep decline in prices in relation to nonalcoholic alternatives at the same time manufacturers were presented with more options to reach and persuade consumers and exhibited a greater willingness to expend corporate resources to do so.

And indeed, alcohol consumption did increase over the period as predicted, Figure 2.7, although perhaps not as much as the cumulative weight of the societal factors might suggest that it should. Total per capita consumption, in fact, was stable at roughly two gallons a year per adult for the first ten years of the study. It rose steadily over the next decade and remained at a plateau of roughly 2.8 gallons per adult per year through 1980. Thereafter consumption declined reaching the historical average of 2.4 gallons per adult per year by the end of the study period.

At the category level, beer consumption remained flat until 1960 accounting for one gallon of absolute alcohol consumption a year through 1965. It then grew by half, reaching a peak around 1980, and remaining at that level for the next decade. On average 1.18 gallons of raw alcohol per adult per year were sourced from beer drinking over the study period. The average consumption from liquor drinking was similar, .948 gallons, but the trend differed markedly. Liquor consumption grew for the first half of the study, alcohol intake rising

Table 6.1
Predicted Effect of Societal Trends on Consumption and Share of Consumption

Trend	Change	Consumption	Share of Consumption
Demographic	Doubling of young adult population	+	+ Beer – Liquor
Economic			
• Income	Personal disposable income doubles in real terms	+	+ Liquor
• Price	Prices halve relative to CPI for other consumer products	+	+ Liquor
Media	Media venues proliferate	+	+ Beer
	Manufacturers increase ad spending		

from .73 to 1.15 gallons, but declined for the last half and had by the end of the study reached its starting level. Alcohol consumption from wine drinking, lastly, averaged .286 gallons per adult per year. Over the study period consumption doubled growing to .4 gallons from .2.

On a share of total consumption basis the big winner over time was beer consumption. Roughly half of all consumption was sourced from beer consumption, 48.9%, while liquor contributed 39.4% and wine 11.7%. But over time, beer share gained ten points growing from 44.5% of total consumption to 54.7%. Wine share also increased sharply, moving from 9.9% to 15.1%. The beer and wine gains were offset by reciprocal losses in liquor share which fell from a 45 share to 31.8.

It is clear then that the four decades from 1950 to 1990 was a period of great social change for the United States. Demographic, economic, and media trends, working together, created an environment that encouraged the consumption of alcohol. The trends did not, however, work uniformly at the beverage category level. Nonetheless, the structural composition of total alcohol consumption did evolve over the period, shifting to beer and wine consumption and away from liquor.

CATEGORY CONSUMPTION

The impact of the underlying societal trends was quantified in a series of regression models. For each of the three forms of consumption, beer, wine, and liquor, two regression models were built. One involved raw data and simply related gross historical trends to one another in a regression context. This analysis provides some insight into how societal trends vary in relation to consumption over time and which social and economic trends are significantly related to consumption when other factors are controlled. The second set of models used transformed data, first differences, in which the annual changes in the variables are associated. First differences focus the analysis on the margin, that is, only that portion of the data that change from year to year. As such, they are less likely to be influenced by long-term historical trends. Advertising ''effects'' observed when first differences are used are more likely to be real, therefore, and we give them more credence when evaluating advertising effects. Results of the regression analyses are given in Table 6.2.

Recall in the raw data model that year measures the linear trend in consumption for the three categories and in this regard the long-term trend for both beer and liquor is toward lower consumption. Recall also that the intercept terms measure the mean consumption, in gallons of raw alcohol per adult per year, for each drinking source and the R^2 statistic measures the percentage of variance in the individual category consumption that is explained by the predictor variables.

With respect to the demand determinants, population operates as expected, increasing beer and wine consumption while depressing consumption of liquor.

Table 6.2
Summary of Significant Predictors of Category Consumption

		RAW DATA			FIRST DIFFERENCES		
		Beer	Wine	Liquor	Beer	Wine	Liquor
	Year	−	NS	−	NS	NS	−
	Population	+	+	−	+	NS	NS
	Income	+	NS	+	NS	NS	+
	Price	−	NS	−	NS	NS	−
Category	Advertising	NS	NS	+	NS	NS	NS
	b_0	1.191	.321	.963	.009	.004	.001
	R^2	.973	.893	.768	.334	.301	.552

Our models confirm the marketing belief that beer and wine to a lesser degree are the preferred alcoholic beverages of the young. Economic variables work as predicted for beer and liquor, consumption rising with greater affluence and with the decline in prices. Advertising is only statistically significant in one model in which increased liquor advertising is associated with greater consumption.

When we examine the first difference model the truly salient drivers of demand are isolated. Beer consumption is directly associated with changes in the young adult population. Liquor is influenced most by economic factors, increasing with gains in affluence and declines in prices. Wine consumption is not significantly related to changes in any of the predictor variables. Most importantly for our purposes yearly changes in advertising are not statistically related to changes in consumption for any of the product categories.

Table 6.3 summarizes the observed advertising effects on category consumption and gives their estimated volumetric consequences. Note that of the six relationships only half are even positive suggesting advertising is associated with increased consumption of a beverage type and, as discussed before, only one is statistically significant (boxed). Since the significant effect for liquor is not confirmed when first differences are used, we must question its validity, although not its direction. The relationship becomes even more suspect when time order is considered, as will be discussed shortly.

One way to look at the strength of the relationship is by the percentage of variance in consumption explained by advertising. Our estimates range from 0 to 11.6%. But the highest value, 11.6% for liquor advertising using raw data has already been questioned. The second highest, 8.8% for wine first differences describes a negative relationship between advertising and consumption. The most reliable estimates for beer and liquor first differences are 1.3 and 2.1% respectively, and these results are consistent with quasi-experimental findings.

If we play through the likely increase in consumption that might accompany greater advertising, only the three positive relationships can be estimated. For these, our model suggests that if magazine advertising spending were to increase by $1 million in real terms for one beverage category only, the incremental consumption per adult per year would range from .02 to .15 gallons or 2.6 to 19.2 ounces. For what we believe to be the best advertising estimates, a million dollars additional spending in magazines would equate to just under three shots of liquor per adult per year or if the spending were for beer, a six pack. Averaged over a year for the entire adult population of the country the figures seem inconsequential, but they may not be if the advertising effect falls differentially on specific subpopulations.

An effort was made to corroborate the advertising effects observed in the regression models. We examined first three alternative ways of defining advertising spending and found either contradictory results for raw data or no statistically significant effects for first differences. We have more reason to question the role of advertising in determining category consumption, therefore, since no

Table 6.3
Advertising Impact on Category Consumption

	Relationship	Variance Explained (%)	INCREMENTAL VOLUME (PER ADULT, PER YEAR) Gallons	Ounces
Raw Data				
Beer	–	–	–	–
Wine	–	.2	–	–
Liquor	+	11.6	.15	19.2
First Differences				
Beer	+	1.3	.05	6.4
Wine	–	8.8	–	–
Liquor	+	2.1	.02	2.6

effects using the broadest definition of advertising including the six major media or total spending were found to be significant for first differences.

Perhaps the final blow to the notion that advertising affects category consumption came when time dependencies were investigated (Table 6.4). We found no instance, raw or first difference, where advertising spending was temporally prior to and hence possibly causally related to consumption. Only one contemporaneous effect was significant, liquor first differences, but as noted above this effect disappeared when other variables were included in a regression model. There is no reason to believe then that advertising spending leads consumption, that is, that advertising spending in one year will affect consumption in subsequent years.

By contrast we do see indications that consumption leads advertising for two beverage categories. In particular, consumption was found to lead advertising by one year for wine and two years for liquor and, importantly, these significant effects were seen for both raw data and first differences. Our results are similar to those reported in the literature (e.g., Duffy, 1990) and support the notion that advertising spending is set in a budgetary context. Past sales of a product are used to predict future receipts and then the amount of advertising spending a company can afford. In an interesting reversal of expectation, consumption determines advertising.

When the findings are considered as a group, we conclude that there is no compelling evidence to suggest that advertising affects category consumption for the following reasons:

1. the one statistically significant relationship for liquor using raw data was not replicated when different advertising specifications, first differences or time dependencies were examined;

2. the effects were inconsistent, for example, directionally half were positive, half negative, and no uniform significant effects were found for different advertising specifications or study time periods;

3. no relationship using first differences, including basic regression models, different advertising specifications or time lags, was found to be significant; and

4. no time lag for raw data or first differences indicated that advertising temporally preceded consumption.

Our only replicable finding is that consumption leads advertising for wine and liquor products and hence past consumption may to a degree determine future advertising.

SHARE OF CONSUMPTION

The findings for share of consumption are virtually a repeat of those for category consumption, with a few minor exceptions. Table 6.5 reexamines the

Table 6.4
Crosscorrelations of Advertising with Consumption

Time Difference		RAW DATA			FIRST DIFFERENCES		
		Beer	Wine	Liquor	Beer	Wine	Liquor
Lead	2	NS	NS	+	NS	NS	+
	1	NS	+	NS	NS	+	NS
	0	NS	NS	NS	NS	NS	+
Lag	−1	NS	NS	NS	NS	NS	NS
	−2	NS	NS	NS	NS	NS	NS

Table 6.5
Summary of Significant Predictors of Category Share of Consumption

	RAW DATA			FIRST DIFFERENCES		
	Beer	Wine	Liquor	Beer	Wine	Liquor
Year	NS	NS	−	+	NS	−
Population	+	NS	−	NS	NS	−
Income	−	NS	+	NS	NS	+
Price	+	NS	−	NS	NS	−
Advertising	NS	NS	+	NS	NS	NS
b_0	48.7	12.3	39.5	.080	.104	−.175
R^2	.678	.838	.900	.534	.186	.629

Category

135

findings of the regression models. As before, the intercept is the mean of the dependent variable so that, for raw data, the historical average beer share of total consumption is 48.7, while liquor and wine shares are 39.5 and 12.4, respectively.

Note in the raw data model since shares always sum to a constant, a gain by one category must be accompanied by a reciprocal loss in the others. As a consequence effects, especially for variables that are constant for all categories, for example, Income, have opposite effects depending on the categories. For instance, growth of the young adult population is associated with higher beer share which, in turn, is garnered from liquor share. Conversely, since liquor is more sensitive to economic variables, its share rises with affluence and falling prices and beer share falls accordingly. This leads to the seemingly paradoxical finding that beer share rises as prices increase when the effect is actually a response to liquor share movement. In sum, the pattern of significant findings for raw data reveals a compensatory share shift dynamic between beer and liquor.

As we saw with category consumption, most significant effects seen for raw data disappear when the data are differenced. Only liquor share is significantly related to the predictors and again share of total consumption represented by liquor rises with greater affluence and falling prices but declines as the young adult population grows.

The pattern of advertising effects are the same as that seen for category consumption. There is a positive and statistically significant relationship between magazine advertising spending and liquor share for raw data but the effect is not present after differences are taken. Using different advertising specifications yields results identical to those for category consumption. No consistent pattern in significant relationships is seen for raw data and no significant effects at all are seen for first differences. Finally, when we examine time order in the data we find again that advertising does not lead share of consumption and, in this instance, that share does not lead advertising. There are, in short, no significant lead or lagged relationships between advertising and share of consumption.

Based on the evidence we conclude that advertising does not significantly impact share of consumption at the category level. We found only one statistically significant finding, and it could not be replicated when the data were differenced or alternative specifications of advertising were used. There are no significant time-ordered relationships, suggesting that if indeed advertising spending levels are set in a budgetary context based on historical performance, the measure used is sales and not share. The findings also suggest that if advertising works profitably for manufacturers it is at the brand level and that any brand specific benefits, when accumulated, are not measurable at the category level.

TOTAL CONSUMPTION

Past econometric work has shown that total alcohol consumption is, in fact, a system of manifest consumer choices among product substitutes. Increased consumption of one beverage type is typically offset by declines in the others such that the overall movement in total consumption is greatly attenuated. Effects seen at the category level for a predictor like advertising are not strictly additive therefore, but rather tend to dissipate across the system of product options. To accommodate systemwide effects in our analysis we combined total consumption with category consumption and share and subsequently related the composite variables to advertising.

Table 6.6 summarizes the results of the investigation of systemwide effects for raw data. Specifically two factor analyses were performed, one combining total consumption and category consumption and the second linking total consumption with category share. The factors were then related to three predictor factors, two of which represented the variability in wine and liquor advertising combined and, second, beer advertising.

For the analysis involving consumption about two-thirds of total consumption variability is explained by wine and beer consumption. This factor is significantly related to wine and liquor advertising such that increases in advertising spending are associated with consumption increases for beer, wine, and in total. Liquor drinking accounts for roughly a third of the variance in total alcohol consumption and this factor is related to both advertising factors. Sensibly enough, liquor consumption and its proportionate share of the total are positively associated with wine and liquor advertising and negatively with the amount of ad spending for beer products.

The second systemwide factor solution involving share of consumption and total isolated three factors. One factor describes the give and take share shifts between beer and liquor presaged by the regression results given in Table 6.5. Wine and liquor advertising is negatively associated with this factor, suggesting that beer gains share from liquor when advertising for wine and liquor products is low. Another factor described variability in wine share exclusively. Because factors are uncorrelated the solitary wine share factor indicates that wine share is largely independent of the beer-liquor trade-off dynamic. Wine share was not significantly related to advertising.

Especially valuable for our purposes, the analysis isolated a pure total consumption factor. The fact that total consumption was not combined with any beverage share suggests that consumption is for the most part unaffected by share shifts between categories. And since the total quantity consumed is not dependent on the mix of its constituent parts, a separate total consumption factor leads credence to the belief that effects at the category level dissipate systemwide.

Interestingly advertising is related to the total consumption factor. Specifi-

Table 6.6
Results of Factor Analytic Regressions for Consumption and Share of Consumption

	CONSUMPTION		SHARE OF CONSUMPTION		
	Beer, Wine & Total	Liquor & Total	Beer (+) vs Liquor (−)	Total Consumption	Wine Share
Trend	+	NS	+	+	+
Wine & Liquor Advertising	+	+	−	+	NS
Beer Advertising	NS	−	NS	−	NS
R^2	.967	.687	.568	.870	.283
Total Consumption Variance Explained (%)	65.6	33.6	.1	96.0	3.6

cally, wine and liquor advertising are positively related to total consumption as they were in the two consumption factor analytic regressions. Similarly, beer advertising is negatively associated with total consumption as it was for the liquor and total consumption factor analytic regression. So for raw data at least, it appears that higher levels of wine and liquor advertising spending in magazines is associated with relatively high levels of total consumption. Conversely, years in which beer advertising is high are years in which total consumption is likely to be low.

And yet these relationships appear to be heavily influenced by the nonstationary aspects of the time series. When first differences are taken the gross trends are removed from the data and not coincidentally advertising effects vanish. Table 6.7, summarizing the two factor analytic regressions using differenced data, illustrates this phenomenon quite clearly. Again, the demand predictors were factor analyzed and three advertising factors, for beer, wine, and liquor, were isolated. The three separate, uncorrelated factors for category advertising enable us to assess the effect of each on total consumption uniquely. As before the outcome variables were factor analyzed one analysis involving consumption, category, and total, and the second including total consumption with share of consumption. The outcome factors were then regressed on the predictor factors.

The factor analysis of consumption revealed that total consumption was proportionately spread across the various categories. About 55% was associated with liquor drinking, 35% with beer consumption, and 11% with wine. When these three factors were regressed on the predictor factors, there was no significant relationship between any consumption factor and any advertising factor.

A similar result was obtained when share of consumption was considered. As before, a three factor solution described the outcome variables. One factor described the beer-liquor share trade-off and another wine share exclusively. Fortunately, the factor analysis also isolated a pure total consumption factor, which when regressed on the three advertising factors, permits a clean test of the relationship between advertising and total consumption. The result once again is clear cut. There is no significant relationship between advertising for any of the three beverage categories and total consumption.

Table 6.8 provides another way to assess the contribution of advertising to total consumption, in terms of the amount of variance explained. The variance in total consumption explained by each factor in which it was involved is in turn conditioned by the variance in the factor explained by advertising (the squared regression coefficient). The end result is the amount of variance in total consumption explained by advertising. To illustrate, liquor consumption explains 54.8% of the variance in total consumption and the coefficient for liquor advertising with the factor is .227. Therefore our estimate for the variance explained in total consumption is 2.82% ($.548 \times 227^2 \times 100$). Notice we have not calculated variance explained figures for negative effects. Finally, since all factors are uncorrelated they are unique and effects can be added across categories to obtain a total advertising effect.

Table 6.7
Results of Factor Analytic Regressions for Change in Consumption and Share of Consumption

		CONSUMPTION			SHARE OF CONSUMPTION		
		Liquor & Total	Beer & Total	Wine & Total	Beer (+) vs Liquor (−)	Wine Share	Total Consumption
Ads	Beer	NS	NS	NS	NS	NS	NS
	Wine	NS	NS	NS	NS	−	NS
	Liquor	NS	NS	NS	NS	NS	NS
Population & Price		NS	+	+	+	NS	+
Income		NS	NS	NS	NS	NS	NS
Trend		−	NS	NS	−	NS	−
Beer Price		NS	NS	NS	NS	NS	NS
R^2		.508	.438	.328	.588	.284	.416
Total Consumption Variance Explained (%)		54.8	34.8	10.9	3.6	−	96.0

Table 6.8
Summary of Variance in Total Consumption Explained by Advertising

	Liquor & Total	Beer & Total	Wine & Total	Total Consumption
Variance Explained By Factor (%)	54.8	34.8	10.9	96.0
Regressior Coefficients				
Beer	−.022	.029	.075	.030
Liquor	.227	.235	−.239	.227
Wine	−.013	.138	−.266	−.001
Variance Explained By Advertising Factor (%)				
Beer	—	.03	.06	.09
Liquor	2.82	1.90	—	4.90
Wine	—	.70	—	—
TOTAL	2.82	2.63	.06	4.99

The results indicated that roughly 5% of the variance in total consumption is accounted for by advertising, either 4.99% for total consumption alone or 5.51% summed across the totals for the three factors. Nearly all of the effect is due to liquor advertising and may, as mentioned often before, be a function of the advertising specification and the disproportionately heavy advertising spending in magazines for liquor products. These figures are very similar to those reported in the literature and obtained from quasi-experimental studies; the range reported in the past based on survey analysis was .2 to 4%. Thus, two very different study designs, data sets, and analytic approaches have come to nearly the same conclusion—we have in the final analysis evidence for a weak, albeit statistically nonsignificant, relationship between advertising and total consumption.

MORTALITY

The last step in our analysis was to estimate the impact of advertising on mortality from alcohol-related disease as it is mediated through total consumption. Three causes of death were selected for study, cirrhosis of the liver with alcohol specified, alcoholism or equivalently alcohol dependence syndrome, and alcoholic psychosis. Unlike other causes of death such as esophageal cancer or traffic accidents for which alcohol use is implicated in only a portion of the mortality rate, the three causes of death chosen for study could be considered to be the exclusive by-products of excessive consumption. As such, they represented the best opportunity to measure an advertising effect on mortality.

Over time the three mortality rates tend to parallel the movement of total alcohol consumption. However, in many instances mortality trends appeared to precede similar movements in consumption. No strong or consistent time dependencies were found when the data were examined for leads and lags or modeled with Box-Jenkins techniques. As a consequence, the analysis was conducted using contemporaneous statistics for advertising, total consumption and mortality.

We first filled in the transitional probabilities of moving from one stage of the conceptual model to the next, Figure 5.3. A base case was then forecast to obtain mortality rates under historical average conditions. Subsequently, we conducted a series of simulations in which advertising and prices were systematically varied. Specifically, we estimated the change in mortality that would occur if advertising were increased by 10% for each of the beverage categories separately and then if all three increased 10% simultaneously. Similar forecasts were run to determine the effect of a 10% decline in individual category prices and then if prices dropped 10% for all beverage classes at the same time. Advertising and prices were chosen for the simulation because it was felt they were the demand predictors that were most directly controllable by legislative bodies.

The results of the simulation expressed as incremental deaths that might occur with changes in advertising or prices are given in Table 6.9. For example a 10% increase in wine advertising might be associated with eight deaths due to cir-

Table 6.9
Predicted Incremental Deaths from Advertising and Price Changes

	Alcoholic Cirrhosis	Alcoholism/ ADS	Alcoholic Psychosis	Total
Base	9,495	3,558	429	13,482
10% Increase in Advertising				
Beer Only	—	—	—	—
Wine Only	8	3	—	11
Liquor Only	206	74	4	284
All Three	210	74	4	288
10% Decrease in Price				
Beer Only	1,011	363	17	1,391
Wine Only	—	—	—	—
Liquor Only	1,507	542	25	2,074
All Three	2,387	1,400	39	3,826

rhosis of the liver above the base number of deaths of 9,495 for this cause. For the same disease a 10% decrease in beer prices is forecast to result in 1,011 additional deaths. A series of specific conclusions can be drawn from the table:

1. beer advertising is unrelated to mortality;
2. the overwhelming majority of the effect due to advertising changes involve spending for liquor products;
3. a 10% increase in advertising for all three beverage categories, nearly 21 million real dollars of magazine advertising in our study, is related to 288 more deaths per year from the three causes;
4. wine price is unrelated to mortality;
5. roughly 40% of mortality increases associated with price reductions are due to beer and 60% are due to liquor;
6. a simultaneous 10% decrease in prices for the three consumption categories is associated with 3,826 extra deaths per year from the three causes; and
7. price reductions are 13 times more influential in affecting mortality when compared with similar proportionate increases in advertising.

These results are bound to be controversial and we repeat they must be considered in light of the limitations of the data and the full compilation of findings. Since the analyses have shown no reliable advertising effects and indeed advertising seems to follow consumption in several cases the deaths associated with advertising changes may be statistical artifacts. The price effects are less easily dismissed.

Another way to look at the simulation results is to estimate the percentage change in consumption, category, and total that would accompany a 10% change in advertising or price (Table 6.10). We can see from the table that a 10% increase in advertising for a category would increase consumption for the same category by 0 to 2.7%. Similarly 10% increases in advertising for all categories would increase total consumption by 1.1%. These figures are remarkably similar to those reported in U.K. econometric studies in which a rough 10:1 ratio was found between advertising and consumption. A 10% increase in advertising finally is predicted to raise total mortality 0 to 2.1% depending on category and 2.1% if advertising for all three beverage classes increases at the same time.

Consumption is much more elastic with respect to price reduction. Category consumption is forecast to rise 5.6 to 19.7% depending on category with a 10% reduction in price. Total consumption should increase .7 to 7.8% again depending on the category for which prices are reduced and 12.3% if the price of all three beverage types drops 10% simultaneously. Total mortality is predicted to increase 10.3% if beer prices decline 10%, 15.4% if liquor prices do, and 24.4% if the price of all products declines 10%. It bears repeating: with equal propor-

Table 6.10
Percentage Change in Consumption and Mortality with a 10% Change in Advertising and Price

INCREMENTAL CHANGE (%)

	Category Consumption	Total Consumption	Total Mortality
10% Increase in Advertising			
Beer Only	—	—	—
Wine Only	.3	0	.1
Liquor Only	2.7	1.1	2.1
All Three	—	1.1	2.1
10% Decrease in Price			
Beer Only	10.7	5.2	10.3
Wine Only	5.6	.7	—
Liquor Only	19.7	7.8	15.4
All Three	—	12.3	24.4

tionate changes price is at least ten times more powerful than advertising in affecting changes in consumption and mortality.

A FINAL SCORECARD

A summary of the major conclusions of the research is given in Table 6.11. When deciding whether to accept or reject the null hypothesis we elected to concentrate on the best evidence for real advertising effects, relationships that are not likely to be artificially inflated by long-term historical trends. The results in the table that refer to statistical tests are based on the analysis of first differences therefore.

The findings demonstrate quite clearly that there is no statistically significant relationship between advertising and any form of consumption including category consumption, total alcohol consumption, or category share of total consumption. Furthermore, this finding is confirmed for every definition of advertising used and time period studied. There is as well no evidence to indicate that advertising temporally precedes consumption; quite the opposite, in two of three cases past consumption appears to help determine current advertising levels. On the strength of these findings we accept the null hypothesis and conclude—advertising has no effect on total consumption of alcohol or rates of morality from alcohol-related disease.

And yet . . . our results do show a consistent, low-level relationship between advertising and consumption and finally mortality. The effects are not statistically significant and normally would be attributed to chance, but they are too similar to findings from other investigations in the field to be ignored, we think. Consistent with the results reported for several quasi-experimental studies our analysis suggests that up to 5% of the variance in total consumption may be explained by advertising. Like econometric estimates of advertising elasticities we find a 10% increase in advertising will raise total alcohol consumption by about 1%. With respect to mortality, advertising was shown to account for roughly 2% of yearly deaths from three alcohol-related diseases, a contribution in line with those reported for other adverse outcomes in quasi-experimental studies.

Our results in conjunction with this multidisciplinary body of evidence do, therefore, lend credence to the notion that advertising contributes, in a very minor way, to total alcohol consumption and negative health consequences associated with excessive drinking. But the relative contribution of price to consumption and mortality also shows, we believe, how minor the advertising role is when compared with other influences that are under the control of policymakers.

Table 6.11
Advertising Effects: A Final Scorecard

	<u>Comment</u>
Category Consumption	Weak, nonsignificant relationship explaining 1.3 – 8.8% of variance in consumption depending on category
	No significant effects regardless of advertising definition
	Past consumption appears to determine current advertising levels for wine and liquor
Share of Consumption	No significant relationships and no time dependencies
Total Consumption	Weak, nonsignificant relationship, explaining no more than 5% of the variance in total consumption
	10:1 ratio observed, i.e., 10% increase in advertising raises total consumption 1%
Mortality	Large increases in advertising associated with small increases in mortality
	10% increase in advertising associated with 2% rise in mortality from selected causes
	Advertising effects are dwarfed by the impact of price changes

Notes

CHAPTER I

1. An illustration of how impassioned the debate about alcoholic beverage advertising can become is shown in the *British Journal of Addiction* editorial (Wallack, 1992) and the various responses to it (Herbits, 1993; Rae, 1993; Mitchell, 1993; Daube, 1993; Gerstein, 1993; Mosher, 1993; Hammersley, 1993; Single, 1993; Hawks, 1993; Mason, 1993).

CHAPTER 2

1. The categories of magazines covered by LNA include: weeklies and biweeklies (e.g., *Time*); monthlies (e.g., *Smithsonian*); women's (e.g., *Cosmopolitan*); home (e.g., *House and Garden*); fashion and service (e.g., *Vogue*); business (e.g., *Forbes*); youth (e.g., *Boy's Life*); outdoor and sports (e.g., *Field and Stream*); and mechanics and science (e.g., *Popular Science*); male-oriented titles (e.g., *Playboy*) are subsumed under monthlies.

CHAPTER 3

1. Due to the limitations of obtaining price data, the consumption series are not equal length, 38 years for beer and liquor and 27 years for wine. As a consequence, the average alcohol consumption figures or intercepts of the three models are not exactly additive and cannot be summed to obtain an average annual total alcohol consumption per adult.

2. To make the coefficient for income the same order of magnitude as the other predictor variables and hence make the regression tables more interpretable, personal disposable income per capita was divided by $10 before entry into the demand model.

3. For a discussion of the effect of multicollinearity on regression models and its impact on social science research see Fisher (1977).

4. All demand models, raw data and first difference, consumption and share of consumption, were also run with beverage share of voice replacing advertising spending. The results did not differ from those obtained using real advertising spending.

CHAPTER 4

1. For a summary of these studies see Table 6.4 in Fisher (1993, p. 138).

CHAPTER 5

1. The 7th version of the international classification of disease (ICD) contained a category with ICD number 322 which was called alcoholism. In 1968 the 8th version of the ICD was introduced and contained a category with ICD number 303, again called alcoholism. No change in definition was made at this time.

In 1979 the 9th version of the ICD was implemented. In the 9th version there is a category 303 called alcohol dependence syndrome (ADS) and a new category—ICD number 305—called non-dependent use of drugs.

Cases in the 8th classification category 303 were split into these two categories in the 9th classification. However, category 305 of the 9th classification contains cases that would have been in categories other than 303 of the 8th classification. This causes a discontinuity in data definition that cannot be adjusted for by aggregation.

At the implementation of the 9th classification, a comparability ratio for category 303 was calculated to be 0.8185. This estimates the instantaneous proportion of ADS cases that were called alcoholism in the 8th classification.

2. Consistent with Box-Jenkins methodology, the raw data series was prewhitened before crosscorrelations were computed.

3. An excellent discussion of the methodological complexities in relating consumption and mortality time series is given in Skog (1980; 1986).

Bibliography

Ackoff, R., and J. Emshoff. (1975). Advertising Research at Anheuser-Busch, Inc. (1963–1968) I. *Sloan Management Review*, 16(2), 1–15.

Adlaf, E. and P. Kohn. (1989). Alcohol Advertising, Consumption and Abuse: A Co-variance—Structural Modeling Look at Strickland's Data. *British Journal of Addiction*, 84, 749–757.

Assmus, G., J. Farley, and D. Lehmann. (1984). How Advertising Affects Sales: Metan-alysis of Econometric Results. *Journal of Marketing Research*, 21, 65–74.

Atkin, C., J. Hocking, and M. Block. (1984). Teenage Drinking: Does Advertising Make a Difference? *Journal of Communications*, 28, 71–80.

Bandura, A. (1965). Influence of Models' Reinforcement Contingencies on the Acqui-sition of Imitative Responses. *Journal of Personality and Social Psychology*, 1, 589–595.

Bandura, A., D. Ross, and S. A. Ross. (1963). Imitation of Film Mediated Aggressive Models. *Journal of Abnormal and Social Psychology*, 66, 3–11.

Cafiso, J., M. Goodstadt, W. Garlington, and M. Sheppard. (1982). Television Portrayal of Alcohol and Other Beverages. *Journal of Studies on Alcohol*, 43, 1232–1243.

Clarke, D. (1976). Econometric Measurement of the Duration of Advertising Effect on Sales. *Journal of Marketing Research*, 13, 345–357.

Clements, R., and E. Selvanathan. (1988). The Rotterdam Demand Model and its Ap-plication in Marketing. *Marketing Science*, 7, 60–75.

Daube, M. (1993). Rhetoric or Realistic Objectives? Commentaries. *British Journal of Addiction*, 88, 14–16.

Duffy, M. (1987). Advertising and the Inter-Product Distribution of Demand: A Rotter-dam Model Approach. *European Economic Review*, 31, 1051–1070.

———. (1989). Measuring the Contribution of Advertising to Growth in Demand: An Econometric Accounting Framework. *International Journal of Advertising*, 8, 95–110.

————. (1990). Advertising and Alcoholic Drink Demand in the UK: Some Further Rotterdam Model Estimates. *International Journal of Advertising*, 9, 247–257.

Engs, R. (1989). Do Warning Labels on Alcoholic Beverages Deter Alcohol Abuse? *Journal of School Health*, 59, 116–118.

Fisher, D. (1980). The Apppeal of Alcoholic Beverage Advertisements to Problem and Nonproblem Drinkers. Ph.D. Dissertation, Rutgers University, New Brunswick, NJ.

Fisher, J. C. (1977). Multicollinearity and the Quality of Social Science Research. Unpublished Doctoral Dissertation, Tufts University, Medford, MA.

————. (1993). *Advertising, Alcohol Consumption, and Abuse: A Worldwide Survey.* Greenwood Press, Westport, CT.

Gerstein, D. (1993). Heart and Heed. Commentaries. *British Journal of Addiction*, 88, 16–17.

Grabowski, H. (1976). The Effects of Advertising on Interindustry Distribution of Demand. *Explorations in Economic Research*, 3, 21–75.

Grube, J., and L. Wallack. (1994). Television Beer Advertising and Drinking Knowledge, Beliefs, and Intentions Among Schoolchildren. *American Journal of Public Health*, 84, 254–259.

Hammersley, R. (1993). The Alcohol Industry and Other "Friends." Commentaries. *British Journal of Addiction*, 88, 19–20.

Hawks, D. (1993). What Would a Friendly Alcohol Industry Look Like? Commentaries. *British Journal of Addiction*, 88, 22–23.

Herbits, S. (1993). Problem Solving is Preferable. Commentaries. *British Journal of Addiction*, 88, 9–10.

Kohn, P., R. Smart, and A. Ogborne. (1984). Effects of Two Kinds of Alcohol Advertising on Subsequent Consumption. *Journal of Advertising*, 13, 34–48.

Levy, D., and N. Sheflin. (1985). The Demand for Alcoholic Beverages: An Aggregate Time-Series Analysis. *Journal of Public Policy Marketing*, 4, 47–54.

Lipsitz, A., G. Blake, E. Vincent, and M. Winters. (1993). Another Round for the Brewers: Television Ads and Children's Alcohol Expectancies. *Journal of Applied Social Psychology*, 23, 439–450.

MacKinnon, D., M. Pentz, and A. Stacy. (1993). The Alcohol Warning Label and Adolescents: The First Year. *American Journal of Public Health*, 83, 585–587.

Madden, P., and J. Grube. (1994). The Frequency and Nature of Alcohol and Tobacco Advertising in Televised Sports, 1990 through 1992. *American Journal of Public Health*, 84, 297–299.

Mason, P. (1993). Are Our Friends in the Alcohol Industry There When We Need Them? Commentaries. *British Journal of Addiction*, 88, 23–24.

Mayer, R., K. Smith, and D. Scammon. (1991). Evaluating the Impact of Alcohol Warning Labels. *Advances in Consumer Research*, 18, 706–714.

Mitchell, P. (1993). Why the Alcohol Industry Sticks to Facts, Action, and Commonsense Rather Than Political Rhetoric. Commentaries. *British Journal of Addiction*, 88, 12–13.

Mosher, J. (1993). Implementing Alcohol Policy. Commentaries. *British Journal of Addiction*, 88, 17–19.

Norman, D. (1975). Structural Change and Performance in the Brewing Industry. Ph.D. Dissertation, University of California, Los Angeles.

Ornstein, S., and D. Levy. (1983). Price and Income Elasticities of Demand in Alcohol Beverages. In Galanter, M. and A. Paredes (Eds.), *Recent Developments in Alcoholism Vol. I.* Plenum Press, New York.

Peles, Y. (1969). Economics of Scale in Advertising Beer and Cigarettes. Ph.D. Dissertation, University of Chicago.

———. (1971a). Economics of Scale in Advertising Beer and Cigarettes. *Journal of Business*, 44, 32–37.

———. (1971b). Rates of Amorization of Advertising Expenditures. *Journal of Political Economy*, 79, 1032–1058.

Rae, J. (1993). The Case for Collaboration. Commentaries. *British Journal of Addiction*, 88, 10–12.

Savage, G., F. Rohde, B. Grant, and M. Dufour. (1993). *Liver Cirrhosis Mortality in The United States, 1970-90. Surveillance Report #29.* National Institute of Alcohol Abuse and Alcoholism, U.S. Department of Health and Human Services, Rockville, MD.

Scammon, D., R. Mayer, and K. Smith. (1991). Alcohol Warning: How Do You Know When You Have Had One Too Many? *Journal of Public Policy and Marketing*, 10, 214–228.

Selvanathan, E. (1989). Advertising and Alcohol Demand in the UK: Further Results. *International Journal of Advertising*, 8, 181–188.

Single, E. (1993). Warning: The Alcohol Industry May Not Be Your Enemy. Commentaries. *British Journal of Addiction*, 88, 20–22.

Skog, O. (1980). Liver Cirrhosis Epidemiology: Some Methodological Problems. *British Journal of Addictions*, 75, 227–243.

———. (1986). An Analysis of Divergent Trends in Alcohol Consumption and Economic Development. *Journal of Studies on Alcohol*, 47, 19–25.

Smith, D. (1988). Effectiveness of Restrictions on Availability as a Means of Preventing Alcohol-Related Problems. *Contemporary Drug Problems*, 15, 627–684.

Sobell, L., M. Sobell, T. Toneatto, and G. Leo. (1993). Severely Dependent Alcohol Abusers May Be Vulnerable to Alcohol Cues on Television Programs. *Journal of Studies on Alcohol*, 54, 85–91.

Strickland, D. (1981). The Advertising Regulations Issue: Some Empirical Evidence Concerning Advertising Exposure and Teenage Consumption Patterns. Paper presented at the conference *Control Strategies for Alcohol Abuse Prevention, National State and Local Designs for the 80's*, Charleston, SC, pp. 109–124.

———. (1982). Alcohol Advertising: Orientations and Influence. *International Journal of Advertising*, 1, 307–319.

Wallack, L. (1984). Public Health and the Advertising of Alcoholic Beverages. In Holder, H. and J. Hallan (Eds.), *Control Issues in Alcohol Abuse Prevention: Local, State and National Designs for the 80's.* South Carolina Commission on Alcohol and Drug Abuse, Columbia, SC, pp. 95–107.

———. (1992). Warning: The Alcohol Industry Is Not Your Friend. Editorial. *British Journal of Addiction*, 87, 1109–1111.

Weinberg, R. (1984). *Advertising and Malt Beverage Demand: A Macro Analysis of*

Brewing Industry Expenditures 1947-1983. Weinberg and Associates, St. Louis, MO.

Williams, G., D. Clem, and M. Dufour. (1993). *Apparent Per Capita Alcohol Consumption: National, State, and Regional Trends, 1977–91. Surveillance Report #27.* National Institute of Alcohol Abuse and Alcoholism. U.S. Department of Health and Human Services, Rockville, MD.

Index

Absolute alcohol consumption, 4, 17–18, 37, 44. *See also* Total alcohol consumption

Ackoff, R., 67

Adlaf, E., 90

Adverse outcomes, 92–93, 104, 124, 146; alcohol abuse, 8; alcohol-related health problems, 13; drinking and driving, 8; intoxication, 8, 124; psychological involvement, 8

Advertising: Magazine Pages, 21–22, effects, 64–67, 72, 93–95, 101, trends, 31; magazine spending, 21–22, effects, 35, 49–50, 52–53, 64–67, 70, 80, 82–84, 99–100, 113–118, 120–121, 131–134, 139–140, 142–146, trends, 31, 34, 42, 126; Total Media spending, 22–24, effects, 64–67, 72, 93–95, 101, trends, 32, 35–36, 42, 126; Total 6 Media spending, 22–23, effects, 64–67, 72, 93–95, 101, trends, 32, 42. *See also* Magazine Pages; Magazine spending; Total Media spending; Total 6 Media spending

Advertising awareness, 11–12

Advertising bans, 12, 120. *See also* Permissible advertising

Advertising elasticities, 13

Age adjusted cirrhosis mortality rates, 1934–1990, 109–111

Aggression, 2

Alcohol commercials, 6–8, 10, 124

Alcohol consumption, 23, 25; trends, 37–40, 41, 44, 126–127

Alcohol conversion factors, 17

Alcohol dependence syndrome (ADS). *See* Alcoholism

Alcohol expectancies, 12

Alcohol images in mass media. *See* Empirical studies

Alcoholic psychosis, 14, 17, 104; crosscorrelation with consumption, 107–108. *See also* Alcohol-related diseases

Alcoholism, 14, 17, 103, 104, 150; crosscorrelation with consumption, 107–108; trends, 104–107. *See also* Alcohol-related diseases

Alcohol-related diseases: alcoholic psychosis, 104, crosscorrelation with consumption, 107–108, trends, 104–107; alcoholism, 104, 150, crosscorrelation with consumption, 107–108, trends, 104–107; cirrhosis with alcohol specified, 104, crosscorrelation with consumption, 107–111, trends, 104–107; esophageal cancer, 119, 142; traf-

About the Authors

JOSEPH C. FISHER, president, InterData Inc., is an advertising executive and sociologist who has studied alcoholism at length. He is the author of *Advertising, Alcohol Consumption, and Abuse: A Worldwide Survey* (Greenwood Press, 1993).

PETER A. COOK, vice president, InterData Inc., is a market research professional and statistician who has 25 years experience evaluating marketing programs and advertising. He is a specialist in econometric modeling and time series analysis.